Instructions for using AR

LET AUGMENTED REALITY CHANGE HOW YOU READ A BOOK

With your smartphone, iPad or tablet you can use the **Hasmark AR** app to invoke the augmented reality experience to literally read outside the book.

1. Download the **Hasmark app** from the **Apple App Store** or **Google Play**

2. Open and select the (vue) option

3. Point your lens at the full image with the and enjoy the augmented reality experience.

Go ahead and try it right now with the Hasmark Publishing International logo.

MONEY LOCATES YOU
YOUR GUIDEBOOK TO CREATING TRUE RICHES IN YOUR LIFE

Endorsements

"This is an extraordinary book that overdelivers in simplicity and understanding. You will love the philosophy, spirituality, and practical exercises that help you connect to all the abundance you desire. I truly believe your life will be enriched by following this sage advice."

—Peggy McColl,
New York Times Bestselling Author

"Joan provides a clear road map to abundance in a book that is bursting with interesting ideas and practical takeaways. Everyone should own a copy!"

—Judy O'Beirn,
President of Hasmark Publishing International

"Joan's story is inspiring and the energy she exudes and talks about in this book was immediately apparent the first time I met her. Many people are raised to believe they can never have financial abundance and that seeking wealth is wrong. Joan shatters both these myths in her book and shows the connection between the law of attraction, religion, and wealth and how every one of us can transform our lives to be abundant. If your desire to live a spiritual life is holding back your desire to attract wealth in your life, you need this book!

—Kyle Boeckman,
Financial Freedom Expert and
Bestselling Coauthor of *Make Your Kids Millionaires*

"If you are looking to attract more wealth and money in your life, this book is for you. I enjoyed the workbook format that forced me to stop and think about what I had read. I also really enjoyed the tools provided! I read *Money Locates You* and did the exercises and ended up with a feeling of renewed energy and power. A must-read if you truly want results!"

—Gisele Maxwell,
Scientist, Businesswoman,
Business Coach and Bestselling Author
of *Free and Rich Beyond Wealthy*

This book is a profound guide for developing a strong positive relationship with money and generating all of the prosperity you desire and deserve. Joan does an excellent job of conveying the principles for building a successful and wealthy person's Self-Identity. It will help you achieve greater success. Follow these guidelines, and you'll be well on your way to becoming the winner you were meant to be! I strongly suggest that you read it!

—Vladimira Kuna,
High Performance Mindset Coach and
International Bestselling Author
of *The Bible of the Masterminds*

MONEY
LOCATES YOU

*Your Guidebook to Creating
True Riches in Your Life*

JOAN EKOBENA

Hasmark
PUBLISHING
INTERNATIONAL

Hasmark Publishing
www.hasmarkpublishing.com

Permission should be addressed in writing to support@premieredestiny.com
Editor: Judith Scott Judith@hasmarkpublishing.com
Cover Design: Victoria Davidson victoria@killercovers.com and
          WaQas waqas@bookcoverartist.com
Book Design: Amit Dey amit@hasmarkpublishing.com

ISBN 13: 978-1-77482-125-1
ISBN 10: 1774821257

Hasmark
PUBLISHING
INTERNATIONAL

Dedication

To my husband, for your love, insight and support.
I love you.

Table of Contents

Foreword

For the past twenty-five years, I have been on a relentless mission to change the conversation about money and empower people around the world to become millionaires. In this time, I have met and read many books from people claiming to be "experts" in money and wealth creation, but in reality, only a small few have actually walked the walk. Among those few is Joan Ekobena.

The first time I met Joan, I was blown away by her intense passion to empower individuals and positively shift their mindsets when it comes to the topics of money and creating wealth. Her own personal journey from very humble beginnings to building and running an extremely successful multimillion dollar business provides not only inspiration, but a blueprint for success.

From your mind to your hand, Joan's spiritual approach will not only teach you how to create financial abundance, but her ideas and principles can be applied to any area of your life to create even greater abundance, joy, and fulfillment.

So, if you're ready, I urge you to grab your favorite pen and notebook, because this book is jam-packed with ideas, principles, and Laws that you are going to want to note. As I mentioned, Joan is truly a product of her product. Her unique approach to money and wealth creation is one for the ages. The amount of incredible value I received is life changing. I am excited to see how it changes yours.

Loral Langemeier, Money Expert
New York Times Bestselling Author

Preface

You may have been, like me, working very hard, exchanging time for money and not realizing any significant shift in your experiences with wealth. The paycheck was great but not enough to trigger a quantum leap in lifestyle, or your experiences with abundance may have been sporadic. My motivation for writing this book is to show you how you too can achieve an ever-flowing supply of money into your life continuously. *Money Locates You* is the product of the product. That is, the application of the ideas and principles in the book (the product) led to the realization of the book itself (the product). The principles and laws described in the book are based on Truth, and they work! You will learn how to position yourself emotionally, physically, and spiritually to receive the abundance that is forever seeking to come to and through you. Money will locate you for any good Desire if you stay conscious of these Truths and remain vibrationally aligned with the Source of All. Every chapter builds on the preceding one, so I recommend that you read the chapters in sequence to the end for a comprehensive and practical understanding of how to manifest money in ways that you may have once considered impossible.

Acknowledgments

To my dear mother, Deaconess Kate Nguini Fouda, my constant spiritual and emotional support, your unwavering love, words of encouragement, continuous prayers, and blessings have been incredibly helpful in bringing this book to reality.

To my wonderful and dear husband, Paul Tembunde, to whom I have dedicated this book, thank you for bringing me into a new season and phase in my life. Thank you for your confidence in me and your insight, understanding, and support, which helped me create this book.

To my loving children, Wesley, Yazmeen, and Murielle Tembunde, and my niece, Cecilia Molungu, I offer a heartfelt "thank you" for the blessings you are to me. I could devote more time to writing because of your understanding and support. You became my in-house editors and graphic designers. Thanks for your help.

I'm grateful for my family and friends, but I'm even more appreciative to those who responded to the money survey. Thank you for your help in making this book a better version of itself by adding your own beliefs, experiences, feelings, and knowledge.

For Pastor Sola Akinlade, who blessed me daily and nourished my inner man with every positive and encouraging word of Truth, I am eternally grateful.

To Deacon Chris Adjagba, thank you for your continuous spiritual encouragement and practical advice in writing this book. I am grateful to you for my own personal affirmations that helped me reach the finish line.

Thank you, Peggy McColl, my coach and mentor, for your unique technique of bringing out the best in every individual. The title of this book made me shiver with excitement, and those goosebumps you experienced on hearing it gave me the green light to continue. The fire that your initial comments kindled in me to want to become an author has yet to burn out.

This stunning presentation is now in your hands thanks to the expertise and professionalism of Judy O'Beirn and her incredible team at Hasmark Publishing.

And to you, my readers, thank you for buying and reading my book.

Introduction

————— ～ —————

My very humble beginnings fueled the Desire to make money—and a lot of it. When you grow up on the poor side of town and live in a home that is literally falling apart, your money beliefs and your relationship with money can be negatively skewed. Lack was the prevailing keyword whenever money was mentioned. I felt the only way to live a better life was to have money. I was determined to make a lot of it. At the very tender age of eight, I was in business! That's right! I sold every fruit that was in season and made snacks to sell to my schoolmates at lunch break. This Desire to make a lot of money followed me through all of my school years. I did not see any evil in money. I saw only the better lifestyle I could afford the more of it I had.

Many like myself were conditioned to believe that graduating from college, especially completing postgraduate studies and getting a high-paying job, was the most guaranteed path to making a great deal of money. There is absolutely nothing wrong with that, and I am a product of this belief. Growing up, becoming a bank manager was my Desire and goal. I suppose in my young Mind, I assumed the banker had access to all the money in the bank and was, by default, the richest person in town. Little did I know how far from the Truth that was. This perception shaped my reality. My perception evolved to some degree, and I graduated with a postgraduate degree in international banking and finance.

The Desire for money for the betterment of your life and the advancement of humanity is indeed noble and natural. Nothing is wrong with the Desire to have money, and nothing is wrong with desiring it in abundance. It's your birthright.

Now, how you go about its acquisition is a different matter. My upbringing and my environment impressed upon me the importance of education and hard work as the most certain or guaranteed path to financial success. It later became apparent to me that this was the standard expectation in many other parts of the world. A 2014 Pew Research Center survey found that 73% of Americans believed that hard work is key, and it was deemed very important in getting ahead in life financially. You work hard and exchange time for money. Making a great deal of money will then depend on how hard you are able to work and for how long. Undoubtedly, working hard for money has led to the realization of many dreams. Because time is limited, and we have no more than 24 hours a day and 365 days a year, our ability to make money will also be limited by the amount of time we work. To make more money, you have to work even harder and for longer hours. If you are fortunate, you may earn a significant raise or a promotion.

It was the April Fool's Day snowstorm of 1997, and I remember driving to work in the inclement weather. It had snowed heavily, and a memo had gone out asking employees, except for essential employees, not to show up for work. I was not considered an essential employee. I was heavily pregnant with our second child, but neither the pregnancy nor snow stopped me from going to work. I still vividly remember the startled look on my supervisor's face as he asked, "How on Earth did you get here?" I was a hard worker; it had been ingrained in me, and my mindset of time for money was set.

I had the postgraduate degree, and I worked hard, long hours, overtime, weekends, and holidays. I earned raises and was promoted. I made good money, at least in my opinion at the time, but I was trying to locate money the best way I knew how. It's perfectly natural to think that you need to work hard for money, but solely focusing on this belief might result in unrealized potential and the leaving behind of unimaginable riches. Money can actually come to you effortlessly and in abundance. It will locate you if you strictly apply the principles and suggestions discussed in this book. The reason is the simple Truth that these principles work. They have worked for many others, including me, and as long as they are applied correctly, they'll work for you too because money does not discriminate!

So, get ready to be transformed from the inside out as we uncover some infallible and uncommon Truths that will eradicate some old money beliefs and paradigms and catapult you to unfathomed heights.

As you read this book, let the eyes of your understanding be enlightened to see differently, think differently, and live differently forever after. I woke up to a different reality and dared to believe and implement the principles discussed here to accomplish many goals in my life, including owning and operating a successful multimillion dollar company. It is therefore my greatest Desire that as you read my book, *Money Locates You*, you will encounter several *ah ha* moments that will get the wheels of your Mind in motion to transform your life for good! Moreover, I hope these principles will speak to your spirit, your inner man, to inspire and whirl up in you the unstoppable Desire to manifest that which is rightfully yours—*abundance*.

In the following four chapters of part one, you'll learn about some key concepts that are fundamental to comprehending the principles and laws for the manifestation of anything you want, including money.

PART 1

CHAPTER 1

Money, Money, Money

—◆—

"All money is a matter of belief."

—Adam Smith

My younger brother, who was six years old at the time, was perplexed when his mother couldn't buy him the most recent version of his favorite video game. After many unsuccessful attempts, he finally asked, "But Mama, why can't you just go to that box on the wall and get money?" He was certain that money was easy to come by. There was cash in the box on the wall, and all you had to do was go there and take it out. Because he had seen it work for others, his belief that money would be easy to obtain remained unshakable. It had previously worked for others, so why not his mother? This chapter discusses beliefs about money, how those beliefs affect your relationship with money, and, ultimately, how money manifests in your life. But first, we'll take a look at the definition of money, just so we have the same understanding of what money is. There are several definitions of money, including, but not limited to, the following:

- Something generally accepted as a medium of exchange, a measure of value, or a means of payment—*Merriam-Webster Dictionary*

- A current medium of exchange in the form of coins and banknotes; coins and banknotes collectively—*Google Dictionary*

Money, in its simplest form, is a medium of exchange with a generally accepted value for the acquisition of goods and services. As straightforward as these definitions may seem, people have developed many different beliefs about money. The more money you have, the more purchasing power you have. This may seem a good thing to some, who believe with more money they can secure financial freedom, among other things. However, there are those who believe money is evil, and the pursuit of money is the root of all evil. Many people would love to say that money isn't important, that money doesn't matter, that it never makes any difference. They feel money causes great inequalities in the world because those with more money than they know what to do with try to accumulate even more money! Thousands of authors on hundreds of different topics over hundreds of years have explained this. But many people still believe money is everything and refuse to see it as anything less than godly.

I decided to find out what those close to me, as well as certain acquaintances, believed and felt about money. So, I conducted a simple survey with two questions:

- What are your thoughts about money?
- What is your response to the statement "Money locates you"?

I was surprised by the responses, especially to question two. I was also intrigued to see some of the positive remarks about money. I found the answers very insightful because we all think we know what other people might say, but we really don't until we ask them. This example is typical of how people are hesitant to express their real feelings and opinions on certain topics or issues, but when they are prompted, and they do express themselves, much is revealed.

Name	What are your thoughts about money?	What is your response to the statement: Money locates you?
Rebecca	Money can bring bad luck sometimes.	I don't know if I want money to follow me.
Dorothy	Wealth is the ability to fully experience life.	Money does not locate you. You have to locate money.
Kate	Money is a necessity!	I call it forth in the Name of Jesus and it locates me.
Toni	Money has a double face; on one side it is controlled by evil actions and on the flip side it is controlled with positive actions. Money has lots of power, one way or another.	I partially believe in this. I believe one locates money, but I also feel that for some, money follows them.
Judith	Money is the center of confusion in most homes though it is a necessity of life	Am not sure but I think it means money finds you
Simon	Security for a better feature	I don't think so
Beatrice	People say money doesn't but happiness, but I think it does to an extent. Money runs the world we live in now and there's really nothing anyone can do about it.	I don't know what this means.
Mary	Money solves problems and makes enemies	Yes. When you work hard.
Darlene	Useful but should not be the most important thing	False
Marie	Makes life easier to live	No

Chelsea	Money is very important in life because it allows you access to many things such as good healthcare, good food, social activities. The less money you have, the poorer your standard of living will be. A poor standard of living can also shorten your life span in some cases such as if you can't afford access to good healthcare or gyms. The more money you have I believe the more 'comfortable' your life will be.	Personally, I believe I attract an abundance as wealth, money will always locate me no matter what. I work as hard as I can, but I do not stress about where I will have money to buy 'this' or 'that' because I know the doors will open when the time is necessary. For example, instead of stressing about how I will afford to enjoy summer or a holiday, I know doors will open for me to fund it like a new job. Even if I don't get a new job money or opportunities to make money will still locate me by another means.
Sarah	Money can buy you all the luxuries things but can never buy life and happiness	I think if you are ambitious, and you work very hard
Cheryl	I think that money should be invested and enjoyed.	Amen
Cecilia	Money gives one the power to bless others thus money in the right hands leads to a lot of good; solves problems, changes people's lives, brings happiness and much more.	My God shall supply all your needs according to his riches in glory by Christ Jesus. My source is in the word of God. Money locates me because financial prosperity is my birth right and God's blessing is upon my life as well as the Abrahamic blessing: so, I am fruitful and productive. Everyone who is born again is blessed thus money locates me Because God wants me to prosper all the time, I will always be prosperous. I walk in abundance be it in my finances and every aspect of my life.

Jose	Good	Yes
Chantal	It answereth all things but it's not to be loved.	You work to get money; it could be working for yourself or someone. God has blessed our hands and given us the power to get wealth.
Paul	It does as long as I am doing things in the right way.	I LOVE IT! ENJOY HAVING LOTS OF IT ALWAYS!!
Immon	It is not about how much money you have it is about how wisely you use it	Work hard and put effort into things you do to get the things you deserve
Susan	Solves Problems	Never. You earn money. It doesn't just locate you.
Wesley	My response to that is "correct". For me, I expect money to find me. Not because it's needed for everyone and so it should fall into my lap at any time, but because I know I put in work to get what I need, especially if my back is against the wall in regard to the situation I'm in.	I see Money as a tool. One of the most useful, if not the most useful when it comes to outside of one's self in relation to their outward community. Like the character of a good person can be around multiple people and have a positive effect on them, I believe that is how Money should be used.
Florence	Yes	Useful in reaching God's people and paying bills
Alobwede	Money is meant for the lucky ones, not how hard working you are.	Money is a means to an end.
Charles	After winning the national lottery, i will say it's true	I think money allows me to be freer

Patience	Money is good, it pays the bills and solves some problems, but it should not be our primary focus.	No. As much as we can't live or function without money, it should not be our reason for living.
Marie-Anne	God gives seed to the Sower (2 Corinthians 9:10)	My flesh will tell you that money is key, money is essential to improve one's standard of living. But if I let my spirit take over, I'll tell you that one cannot have two masters: God and money-mammon (Matthew 6:24). Money should be key to allow one to invest in God's kingdom.
Bismarck	Freedom	Money for time

Table 1: Money beliefs survey

Let's take a look at the beliefs some famous people have had about money. I must admit, some of them had me laughing hard. I had fun reading them. I hope they make you laugh too, although you might think I have a weird sense of humor. That's all right!

"The money you make is a symbol of the value you create." —*Idowu Koyenikan*

"Lack of money is the root of all evil."—*George Bernard Shaw*

"We insist that money is the root of all evil and behave as if it were the source of all good."—*Charles Edward Jerningham*

"Money has never made man happy, nor will it—there is nothing in its nature to produce happiness."—*Benjamin Franklin*

"Money isn't the most important thing in life, but it's reasonably close to oxygen on the 'gotta have it' scale."—*Zig Ziglar*

"Money is 80% behavior, 20% head knowledge. It's what you do, not what you know."—*Dave Ramsey*

"Money moves from those who do not manage it to those who do."—*Dave Ramsey*

"When I was young, I thought that money was the most important thing in life; now that I am old I know that it is."
—*Oscar Wilde*

"To get rich, you have to be making money while you sleep."
—*David Bailey*

"If you don't find a way to make money while you sleep, you will work until you die."—*Warren Buffett*

"Money is a funny thing. The more you care about it the less you have. The less you care, the more you have."
—*author unknown*

"Both poverty and riches are the offspring of thought."
—*Napoleon Hill*

"Money is not the most important thing in life. Love is. Fortunately, I love money."—*Jackie Mason*

"Money is like a sixth sense—and you can't make use of the other five without it."—*William Somerset Maugham*

"Money, if it does not bring you happiness, will at least help you be miserable in comfort."—*Helen Gurley Brown*

"Money is better than poverty, if only for financial reasons."
—*Woody Allen*

"Money is the opposite of the weather. Nobody talks about it, but everybody does something about it."—*Rebecca Johnson*

"A bank is a place that will lend you money if you can prove that you don't need it."—*Bob Hope*

"Money is the best deodorant."—*Elizabeth Taylor*

"Money is like manure. You have to spread it around or it smells."—*J. Paul Getty*

"Money often costs too much."—*Ralph Waldo Emerson*

"The waste of money cures itself, for soon there is no more to waste."—*M. W. Harrison*

"Money isn't everything, but it's a long way ahead of what comes next."—*Edmund Stockdale*

"Money is not everything. Make sure you earn a lot of it before speaking such nonsense."—*Warren Buffett*

"The money you have gives you freedom; the money you pursue enslaves you."—*Jean-Jacques Rousseau*

"Money may be the husk of many things but not the kernel. It brings you food, but not appetite; medicine, but not health; acquaintance, but not friends; servants, but not loyalty; days of joy, but not peace or happiness."—*Henrik Ibsen*

"The ultimate purpose of money is so that you do not have to be in a specific place at a specific time doing anything you don't want to do."—*Naval Ravikant*

"Money is humankind's greatest invention. Money doesn't discriminate. Money doesn't care whether a person is poor, whether a person comes from a good family, or what his skin color is. Anybody can make money."—*Takafumi Horie*

You may or may not agree with any of these quotations, and that's OK. Later in the chapter, you'll have the opportunity to state your views and beliefs. Some of these beliefs may be positive, while others may be outright negative and limiting. A deeper understanding of your money beliefs, as well as how you interact with money, is an excellent place to start a new journey and have a more prosperous relationship with money. You may be contemplating your own money ideas in your head right now, and you're starting to get the picture. It is important to be very aware of your thoughts and beliefs about money. If you think your beliefs are limiting, this awareness or recognition should not be cause for criticism or discouragement. Rather, awareness presents opportunities for change that could steer your life in a better direction, if you deem it necessary.

The dictionary definition of *paradigm* is a system of assumptions, concepts, values, and practices that constitutes a way of viewing reality. It is a widely accepted belief or a way of looking at something. These beliefs may not necessarily be based on Truths. People's paradigms are formed based on their experiences and the information they receive—what they see and hear from their parents, family members, teachers, religious community, workplace, and so on. Here are some examples of paradigms:

- You can't earn money by doing what you love.
- The rich only get richer and the poor get poorer.
- You don't deserve to be rich because others are struggling.
- People are born into their place in society, so what they become is not up to them.
- Certain positions are reserved for certain social classes.

Limiting beliefs are thoughts, opinions, or convictions that you think are Truths. They instill fear, sometimes create anxiety, and may be the reason for you being unnecessarily cautious.

Not all limiting beliefs are bad. A good limiting belief is one that prevents you from doing something unethical or illegal. If you believe shoplifting is wrong, this belief will prevent you from breaking the law or committing a crime. That's an excellent limiting belief to have.

On the other hand, limiting beliefs based on false opinions or thoughts hold you back from doing the very things you need to do to advance and succeed in life. They actually make it impossible for you to manifest financial abundance. You find yourself unwilling to embark on certain projects, travel to certain places, apply for certain jobs, fall in love with and even marry certain people, live in certain parts of town, go to certain schools, take advantage of certain opportunities—all because of your beliefs about them. You do not even think of doing certain things because you believe they are too difficult, or you won't succeed, or it's flat out wrong for you to embark on them. This mindset will continue to hold you back until you discover how to dissolve the false beliefs that are holding you back. You must shift your perspective on these beliefs if they are causing you to sabotage yourself. Accept something new and fresh into your life's mindset. You must shift your perspective now, or it will still be limiting your life in the future.

The limiting beliefs that we hold with respect to money must be overcome, dissolved, and released into the light of our consciousness so that we can create a new reality for ourselves. What do I mean by this? Well, most people who want to attract more money and experience financial abundance have limiting beliefs about the process of attracting money. To understand the possibility of money locating you, you must understand its role in God's plan for humanity and in your life because God uses money as a tool in creating and manifesting your good Desires.

If you're old enough to remember pop music from the early 1970s, the title of this chapter is sure to bring back memories of ABBA, one of Sweden's most popular bands during that time. Oh, how I love ABBA! Their hit song "Money, Money, Money" was released in 1976, just around the time I was getting ready to go to secondary school. My mom, who lived in France, had come back home for vacation, and she was a real

ABBA fan! As we sat under an orange tree at the back of our house listening to ABBA, the song started playing. Given my experiences then with not having money and my determination to make a great deal of it, the connection was immediate; I fell in love with the song and, of course, the group ABBA. Back then, we had our own songbooks, which were intricately and beautifully hand-drawn and decorated. We would brag to our pals how many songs we had in our songbooks. To write down accurate lyrics, I had to rewind the tape several times. Today, with a quick Google or YouTube search, you'll find the lyrics to almost any song.

In ABBA's song "Money, Money, Money," the group shared its beliefs about money: To obtain it involved working all night and day simply to pay the bills with nothing left for yourself. The strategy, I assume, was to marry a rich guy so that you didn't have to work at all. Accomplishing many things was possible only in the rich man's world where it was always funny and sunny. (Throughout this book, I sometimes use *man* generically to mean humanity or humankind, not literally the male gender.)

My strategy was not to marry a wealthy man (again, nothing wrong with that). My plan was to go to school and work hard. That's what I was told, that's what I saw others do, and it worked for them. I believed money was only for some, the rich or those born with a silver spoon in their mouths.

Your Relationship with Money

Positive thoughts and experiences are the foundation of successful relationships. Whether these thoughts come from experiences in your own life, the world around you, your childhood, news media coverage, or random strangers, they have planted ideas in your Mind that have affected your beliefs and hence your connection with others, things, concerns of life, and money. Money has energy, and it is drawn toward individuals who have positive beliefs about money. Negative beliefs generate negative and limiting ideas. They do more to keep money away from you than to bring it closer to you. If your relationship with money is far from positive, your thoughts and beliefs may be the only thing standing in the way of you making more money.

If you speak to people who have successful businesses, they will tell you success takes much more than just getting an education and working hard at the business. So, what then is the difference between the people who succeed and the ones who don't? There are many differences. People who have successful businesses have a more positive relationship with the idea of making money. Such relationships originate from their beliefs about money.

"Money is a living entity, and it responds to energy exactly the same way you do. It is drawn to those who welcome it, those who respect it. Wouldn't you rather be with people who respect you and who don't want you to be something you're not? Your money feels the same way."—*Suze Orman, The 9 Steps to Financial Freedom*

According to the Law of Attraction, you attract that which you focus on and focus on consistently. Whatever you give your energy to will be attracted to you.

Some of the negative or more limiting beliefs center around money being evil or the root of all evil. They are the basis of many money paradigms that have held many captive and limited their ability to manifest the abundance of money in their lives. The Desire for money at the expense of others is unethical. What is evil is taking from others what is rightfully theirs and doing evil things with money.

Your thoughts, ideas, and beliefs about someone or something have a significant impact on your relationship with that person or thing. I registered for a program by international best-selling author and renowned coach, Peggy McColl. In one of the sessions, she asked the students to take a moment to think about their relationship with money. I must admit that the suggestion seemed strange to me because I had never seriously given any thought to my relationship with money. She took the exercise even further, asking us to write a love letter to money. At that point I just burst out laughing, and I thought she was pushing it. Why? Although I love money, I had never consciously thought about expressing my love for money, let alone been compelled to write about my relationship with money. I'd never wanted to be misunderstood for loving money more than God. It's vitally important to mention here that we should not love money above God. My new awareness and openness to change allowed me to write my love letter to money in no time. Also, I reasoned I'd paid for the course, and if I wanted my expectations to be fulfilled, it was up to me to keep an open Mind and follow the instructions. Below is the first and unedited version of my letter to money.

Dear Money,

How wonderful to finally have you in my life! You kind of eluded me for a long time and today you have shown up in abundance as if apologizing for avoiding me for such a long time. It is indeed amazing to see you at every corner I turn. We have started a beautiful and lasting relationship. You come readily and with free will even without me calling on you. I love that you have found me to be a great partner and together, we'll do many things I never dreamt of. You enjoy that I put you to work for many great causes and you willingly multiply yourself, ready for our next project.

Our love is mutual and continues to eternity.

Your best friend,
Joan
I hope you will enjoy the thrill of writing your own letter to money.

Chapter 1 Exercise: Money Beliefs

Now it's your turn to respond to the two survey questions at the beginning of chapter one. I encourage you to be as true to yourself as you can.

What are your thoughts about money?

_____

_____

_____

_____

_____

_____

What is your response to the statement "Money locates you"?

_____

_____

_____

_____

_____

Your love letter to money:

_____

_____

_____

_____

_____

If you believe money is only for a certain class or there's only so much of it to go around, your thoughts about money will probably center around lack accompanied by excuses as to why you don't have money (or more of it).

If you believe there is enough money out there for anyone who wants it for the right reasons, and you focus your thoughts on the wonderful things you can accomplish with it, money will be drawn to you. Money is constantly circulating. It goes to the person who passes it along and increases it by putting it into action. In the biblical parable of the talents, a master was going on a journey. He gave five talents to the first servant, two to the second, and one to the third. The servant who had five talents traded with them and doubled his money. So did the one who had two talents. However, the servant who received just one talent, dug a hole and buried it away. When the master returned, he was pleased with the two servants who had invested and earned more money. He rewarded them appropriately. However, the third servant did not even attempt to improve his talent or use it for anything. As a result, the master took that ability away from him and gave it to the servant who now had ten talents. The parable of the talents is often taught with an emphasis on using what we've been given and increasing our abilities. This may be a worthy lesson, but there's another lesson that's largely ignored: "For unto every one that hath shall be given, and he shall have abundance: but from him that hath not shall be taken away even that which he hath"—*Matthew 25:29*.

When we do not improve or use what we already possess, it will also be taken from us. This principle expects us to circulate and increase money.

Whether your beliefs are positive or limiting, they are what they are. Do not let that bother you; it is simply what it is. Knowing yourself is not a curse; it is a gift. Self-acceptance, not self-blame, is the path to self-healing. As you continue reading, you'll become more exposed to empowering Truths about money. All that is needed is your willingness and consistency in implementing and practicing the principles and suggestions in this book.

CHAPTER 2

Awareness

———— 🙞 ————

"And ye shall know the Truth,
and the Truth shall make you free."

—*John 8:32*

It all begins with awareness. Awareness is a state of being conscious, having knowledge or perception of a situation or Fact. You may be completely oblivious to what you're not aware of, even if it is in front of your eyes. Lack of awareness can often lead to lack of information or lack of knowledge, which causes many problems because it becomes ignorance. That's how powerful awareness really is! Money, as we all know it today, is in the form of notes and coins. The days of trade and barter are long gone. You can readily accept the idea that money in the form of coins, a piece of metal, has energy, and it can produce sound. It may be more difficult for you to accept and appreciate the concept that even bank notes have energy. If you are aware that money, no matter what its form, has energy, you will quickly accept and believe that it will gravitate toward and locate you.

Awareness is important because without awareness, nothing else matters. Awareness ranges from what you are aware of and the degree to which you are aware of it. Your level of awareness doesn't affect only the quality of what you're aware of, it affects everything. It will determine whether what you are aware of is real or not.

Daily, you are aware of your surroundings, environment, people, thoughts, and items. You are aware of a plethora of things that don't even matter to you. But have you ever given any real thought to asking yourself if you truly know what you're aware of or how much awareness you have of it? We perceive and experience the world through our senses of sight, smell, taste, hearing, and touch. This is the awareness of Facts and natural or manufactured things with which we come into contact in day-to-day life. Without this awareness you wouldn't know what to look for, nor would you be able to recognize what you are looking for with any of your senses.

When you're going somewhere new, especially at night, you check around to ensure that no one is lurking nearby who may be up to no good. In certain cases, for example, if you notice anything strange while trying to get gas, you might go to another station. You may think of this as a split-second awareness of your environment. This generally happens very swiftly, almost on instinct or inadvertently. Sometimes, you may find yourself so absorbed in something that you don't pay attention to others, what's going on around you, or even yourself! This is a lack of awareness. You also may find yourself lacking in awareness if you become engrossed in something that you enjoy very much, such as a television program or a favorite song! In those cases, you're totally unaware of everything else going on around you or even inside your own body! At that moment, you do things absentmindedly. You're on the phone while looking for it in your handbag, for example. I've had to reverse course after driving a few miles to check my garage door, which I normally close as part of my routine. I was not completely present or aware of what I was doing at the time.

To take advantage of or profit from something, you must be aware of it. You may have been keeping an eye on a certain item for a long time, perhaps a pricey designer item from your favorite store, waiting for it to go on sale. The store decides to promote that item, but because you are not aware of the promotion, you are unable to take advantage of it. A story is told about a poor villager who received a million-dollar check from a prominent and wealthy city dweller. He didn't know a check could be cashed for cash, so he framed it and exhibited it in his living room. He wanted to demonstrate to his visitors that he was a genuine fan of the prominent man by displaying his autograph. It was only after a visitor from the city explained to the villager what he had been given that he realized what it was. Unfortunately, the check had passed its expiration date. Is there any sense in having knowledge if you don't utilize it? According to the Small Business Administration, all 2021 Paycheck Protection Program (PPP)-approved lending as of May 31, 2021, was at 6,681,929 loans, worth $277,700,108,079. However, some eligible organizations, particularly small companies, failed to apply for the loan because they were unaware of it or the deadline for submitting an application.

There's also the awareness of Truth at play here. Without the awareness of Truth, you will never be able to perceive anything real. Only with accurate knowledge of what is real can you truly appreciate what's good for you and enjoy your life to the fullest extent possible. Awareness of Truth calls for a deeper and complete sense of awareness. This awareness, which creates conviction, demands an intentional, a conscious, and a wholistic assessment of a person, thing, or situation.

The awareness of Truth allows you to see clearly, which will allow you to make conscious decisions about the things that you want or don't want in your life. You can then create—without effort—an environment that is wholesome, healthy, and conducive to your success. This will allow you to enjoy everything that you want with the people you love! Without the awareness of Truth, you're stuck with making decisions based on what's available to your five senses, which at best can be circumstantial evidence. Ultimately, relying on this type of awareness won't help you discover the Truth about anything important in life. It will only lead you further away from the Truth and deeper into the darkness of ignorance, misconception, confusion, pain, frustration, and disappointment, resulting in poor choices, decisions, and outcomes.

Self-awareness

Awareness is the ability to notice everything, including yourself. As much as lack of awareness may result in some unanticipated outcomes, of greater consequence are

- lack of self-awareness and
- lack of awareness of the difference between Facts and Truth.

Self-awareness has been defined as

- "the conscious knowledge of one's own character, feelings, motives, and desires"—*Oxford Languages dictionary*
- "an awareness of one's own personality or individuality"—*Merriam-Webster dictionary*
- "the ability to take an honest look at your life without attachment of it being right or wrong."—*Betty Ford*

Self-awareness is not a call for judgment but an opportunity to discover who you really are. *What matters most is how you see yourself.*

From this picture in which a cat sees the reflection of a lion in the mirror, the following assumptions can be made about the cat:

- It perceives itself to be of the same species as a lion and thus, sees itself as one.
- It believes it has the same talents and abilities as a lion.
- It is convinced that it will one day be able to do what a lion can do.
- It already views itself as a lion; in other words, its transformation is already complete.

Cat sees lion in mirror

Your degree of self-awareness, or lack thereof, is in part a function of deep-rooted beliefs (as mentioned in chapter one), habits, and patterns developed early in life. You developed these primarily at home from family interactions, school, and the people and culture in your environment.

A lack of self-awareness can have even greater consequences, resulting in the unaware living inauthentic, destructive, unfulfilled, and chaotic lives. This lack of self-awareness drives unconscious behaviors and unquestioned beliefs. Lack of self-awareness causes some people to make the same mistakes over and over; they turn to violence or live meaningless lives with little or no progress.

The benefits of self-awareness cannot be overemphasized. This trait allows you to uncover your uniqueness, strengths, and areas of improvement, and to better understand your emotions and what motivates you to do what you do and much more.

It's crucial to recognize, nevertheless, that your physical self-awareness may be your most significant obstacle to creativity and success. This sort of self-awareness may make you feel inadequate and discouraged. Instead of believing in your power to achieve your dreams, you may think about quitting.

Someone may have advised you to "be true to yourself," or if they came from an older generation, advised "to thine own self be true." That is all very nice and proper, but how can you be true to yourself when you don't know who you are? Are you being true to the person in the mirror or to someone else?

The only way to understand yourself is to be completely aware of who you are, and from where you originate. Therefore, the first step to being aware of yourself is to know who you are. In traditional Chinese medicine, everything around you—from your Body, Mind, and Spirit to the world that exists outside of you—is a reflection of you! It's almost like looking into a mirror because everything that exists, exists in some way for yourself. There is no separation of you and the world.

There are numerous self-assessment tools online. Many simply provide you with a platform or system to describe or document trends, behaviors, routines, and ideas in your life that are obvious to you. The most important questions revolve around your thoughts, feelings, hobbies, how you relate to others, how you arrange or organize your life, what others think of you, your personality, beliefs, values, insights, and so on.

The majority of these tests will prompt you with questions such as the following:

- Do you often feel misunderstood?
- Are you an impulsive person?
- Do you prefer structure and routines over spontaneity and surprises?
- Do you have a positive outlook on life?

The question is whether or not these are the only criteria used to determine who you are, making it easy for others to label you. You could be seen as an impulsive person because of your spontaneity, but how impulsively do you operate in your life? You may think you like spontaneity, but do you know how to embrace and utilize it? Do you let the unexpected surprises in life change your direction or goals?

The majority of these self-assessment tools concentrate on the physical and emotional aspects of self at the expense of the spiritual nature of humanity. It's difficult to discover the real you without incorporating spiritual knowledge for a more holistic approach to self-awareness. Spirituality is self-discovered.

This may be a difficult concept to grasp, so I hope this narrative will provide additional insight. The story is told of an eagle that could not fly. A hunter came across an injured eagle and its nest with just one egg beside it. He believed the eagle had a better chance of surviving if kept in the chicken coop, so he brought it home. Unfortunately, soon after the eaglet hatched, the eagle died. The eaglet grew rapidly and began flapping its wings naturally, mimicking the actions of the other birds. When the hunter released the chickens outdoors, some of them would try to fly but could only reach heights of around 10 feet and span distances of up to 40–50 yards. One day, the hunter decided to release the eagle so it could fly away and live in its natural habitat. The eagle, like the chickens, took off but flew only a short distance before landing clumsily on the ground. The hunter tried letting it out on several other occasions, but each time the eagle flew as far as before. It had been trained by observing what the chickens did. Even though it could soar to heights of up to 10,000 feet, it never attempted to fly high! It was ignorant of its inherent nature and talents, and as a result, it spent its life with the chickens on the ground rather than experiencing an eagle's nature and lifestyle, which involves flying high and far, and which commonly symbolizes power and freedom.

Now, let me ask you some questions:

- How do you perceive yourself?
- Do you know who you are deep down in your heart and Mind?
- How do people perceive you?

A more complete self-assessment will assist you in discovering your true potential and building the lifestyle of your dreams. The ability to do so is inside you, and you must unleash it. The eagle was unaware of its strength. It had been conditioned by a lack of self-awareness or limited awareness of self.

- Do you always doubt yourself and your capabilities?
- Do you feel like you are not living up to your full potential?
- Are you afraid of expressing your true self for fear of being judged or ridiculed?

Are these issues hindering you from living life to the fullest? If so, discover the talents that are inside you. Don't let life slip away from you; experience it to the fullest! Do this by becoming aware of your true self and fully utilizing all that resides within you.

Paul the Apostle is a good example of someone who had a clear and complete sense of who he was. He was spiritually aware and aware of who he was spiritually. He said, "Not that we are sufficient of ourselves to think any thing as of ourselves; but our sufficiency is of God"—*2 Corinthians 3:5*. You need to be aware of who you are in the spiritual, for life is spiritual. Self-awareness will not be complete without spiritual self-awareness. You may not be aware of who you are if you don't have this awareness. Man is a spirit originated by God, so he can't completely gain self-awareness without also gaining spiritual self-awareness. That is who you truly are. Your awareness of who you truly are shapes and determines your life and your world. As author Neville Goddard said, "In the state of consciousness of the individual is found the explanation of the phenomena of life." As you progress from half to full self-awareness, you go from a state of fear, hopelessness, or impossibility into one of confidence, hope, and expectancy. You expect things to work for you in a certain way, with ease, because you know who and whose you are.

Neville Goddard often stated that everyone is either living in an awareness or working out of one. When you are working out of an awareness that you do not know your true nature, you are working out of an awareness that is not aware of itself. You see yourself as limited to the physical senses and therefore only aware of what you can perceive with your physical senses. When you are living in an awareness of who you truly are, you live in the realm within—the spiritual awareness where everything takes place first before it happens in the physical world.

You'll be able to tell that you have an eternally powerful spirit inside yourself when you become aware of your spiritual nature. If you don't perceive or detect this internal power, that doesn't mean that it is nonexistent, or it isn't real. You may be aware of hunger but not notice food.

Facts or Truth

The definitions of Fact and Truth are critical to grasp. Understanding the distinction will alter your perspective into conviction. At that point, you will have advanced from being simply informed to being persuaded. There are Facts, and there are Truths. Truth is reality, but not all Facts are Truth. Facts are what we observe in the physical world. Truths are what we infer from them. Facts are evident, whereas Truths are hidden. To uncover the Truth behind the Facts, you must employ a higher faculty of awareness—intuition. In order to discover the good things in life and to be fully aware of them, you need not only your rational Mind but also your intuition—that extra dimension of awareness. Truth is hidden in the Facts until it is revealed by intuition. The person who lacks intuition, sees only the Facts. In a world of so many voices, the Truth sometimes gets lost in the Facts.

A Fact may be a Truth, but it may not be all-time Truth. A Fact is information about a thing, person, circumstance, or an event. The information may change with time, or it may change based on what criteria or standards are used to qualify it as Fact. Truth is unchangeable and absolute; it simply is. On the other hand, Facts are changeable and not absolute; they can be manipulated to give a false representation of reality. On the other hand, Truth is always constant, regardless of the method used to assess its validity as Truth. Truth is the immutable essence of who you really are; it is your Authentic Self. It is the Divine blueprint that originates in God (Infinite Intelligence, Source) and manifests itself in human beings.

Neville Goddard, in his book, *The Power of Awareness*, states, "'I AM' is that which amid unnumbered forms, is ever the same." I AM is God, and the Word of God is Truth: "...thy Word is Truth"—*John 17:17*. *Truth, therefore, is the revealed Word of God concerning you and everything else. It is reality.* Spiritual self-awareness helps you shift your focus from Facts to Truths. *The Truth is what God has said about you in His Word, and it delivers you from the Facts.* The scripture verse, "And ye shall know the Truth, and the Truth shall make you free," (*John 8:32*) did *not* say ye shall know the Facts, and the Facts will make you free. The point here is that, in order to interact with the unchanging essence of I AM, you must consider the Truth rather than the Facts.

The Facts of life will never make you free. Only the Truth hidden within them makes you free. We as people, as human beings, as created in the image and likeness of God, live with a Mind that has been genetically programmed with thousands of beliefs—beliefs about who we are, what we are, and who God is. We have been raised in a society that has made thousands of false assumptions—many unknowingly—about life, religion, politics, and the role religion plays in our lives. We think these assumptions are really just the way things are, and that's just not true!

When a teacher says that a student is not smart, the claim may be based on evidence of poor grades. If the passing grade is 75%, and the student consistently earns 55%, a Fact has been proven. However, the

Truth is that you are smart because you were made by God, and everything He does is perfect. You can see your fulfillment by shifting your attention from the Fact to the Truth of who you really are. The reason we all go through trials and tribulations in our lives is because we choose to believe Facts instead of Truth, which blinds us from seeing our own perfection.

The student, therefore, must acknowledge the Fact while stating and affirming the Truth: "Because I was formed in the image of the All-Knowing God of Infinite Intelligence, I am smart." It is not enough to know the Fact. The fulfillment of anything requires that you re-emphasize it without ceasing until you believe it. Do not let your Mind or another person pollute your mental waters with negativism, doubt, and disbelief. Your Mind needs to be a spiritual temple where God's Truth resides.

Knowledge is required to understand and make sense of Facts. To discover the Truth, you must have knowledge as well as faith in God. Truth is that which agrees with reality. You can have Truth in any area of your life that you know about, but it has no power until it is mixed with faith. When faith refuses to pay attention to, think about, or recognize Facts, those Facts are disregarded and have no power over your life. Facts become real when they are transformed into Truth by faith. You can see and observe a tree, but you cannot experience the spiritual Fact that God is the Tree of Life unless you have faith.

"When men are cast down, then thou shalt say, there is lifting up"— *Job 22:29*. Based on the Truth of this verse, you can also confidently say, "Let the poor say I am rich." This may not make sense to you now because the Facts don't add up, but once you have the faith to face and accept the Truth, everything changes.

If your bank account is overdrawn, it is a Fact that there's not enough money in your account, but the Truth is that you are not poor. The implication here is that, even though things may appear to be bleak, with no indication of getting better, you can still state the Truth. Truth is not based on physical manifestations or sensory perceptions. As weird and incomprehensible as this may sound to you, do not let your senses analyze or try to reason Truth out for you. There are only absolutes in Truth—no maybes and no assumptions. As a result, all uncertainties are removed, and you have complete knowledge. You need to take the steps of faith and walk in them, even though doing so may not make sense to you.

It's critical to be conscious of the distinctions between Facts and Truth. Your awareness and acceptance of Truth will assist you in achieving your goals. As you begin to apply these ideas in your daily life, in your thoughts and speech, you will notice an elevated consciousness of self. You will begin to align your thoughts with the creative process of God, and you will begin to manifest your needs and Desires with ease.

Once Truth becomes your conscious reality, you'll be able to manifest your Desires as you affirm the Truth using the Principle of Affirmation, explained in a later chapter in this book. Affirming the Truth activates the power of the Infinite Intelligence, causing a thing or situation to conform to your declaration. Therefore, stand firm in the Truth as it pertains to that thing or situation. Refuse to be moved by your senses and the Facts of the situation. Refuse to focus on or be dominated by the Facts of your situation. Rather, let the Truth of God be your focus. Fill your ears, eyes, and mouth with it, so *you* can affect any change you desire in your life now.

Chapter 2 Exercise: Who Do You See in the Mirror? Part 1

Stand in front of a mirror (a full mirror is best). Who do you see in the mirror?

_____

Describe the person you see in the mirror.

_____

_____

_____

_____

_____

_____

_____

_____

_____

_____

_____

_____

_____

_____

_____

_____

_____

_____

_____

CHAPTER 3

The Source of All

———— ❧ ————

"For by him were all things created, that are in heaven, and
that are in earth, visible and invisible, whether they be thrones,
or dominions, or principalities, or powers: all things were created by him, and for him."

—*Colossians 1:16*

You can't comprehend or appreciate Truth without a thorough grasp
of the Source and basis of all Truth. To some people, the term Source
evokes a mystical sensation that they are unable to make sense of or
explain. The Source of anything is its origin, where it takes its life or existence from. The origin of anything may be determined by looking at its
Creator or manufacturer. You will not trust the manufacturer's products
if you do not trust the manufacturer. The question of how life began is a
topic of debate. Some people believe in the Big Bang Theory or that life
started as RNA molecules began to self-replicate and evolve, while others believe life came from a Spirit. For some, the origins of life are not as
straightforward due to a wide range of theories and interpretations.

It is, however, my conviction and belief that life comes from a Spiritual
Source, and thus, my belief that life is Spiritual. It is my understanding

that unless you grasp the reality of this Truth, it will be difficult to understand or appreciate any Truth concerning existence. The Spirit is who God is, and if God is all Truth, then anything He does must also have its origin in Truth. I make this statement because I am of the view that neither goodness nor human-made laws can be considered as the Source or standard of Truth. This means that only God's Laws and His ways are good. They alone are perfect and finished. If they are not, then nothing made by humanity will ever be perfect.

Source has been called many names. Perhaps you refer to Source as the Universe, Universal Mind, Allah, a higher power, the Divine, Buddha; I refer to Source as God, the Creator of all things seen and unseen. Therefore, the words "Source" and "God" will be used interchangeably—the Source of all creation, I AM, the energy that makes all things, the Spirit of Infinite Intelligence, the Alpha and the Omega. Wallace D. Wattles, in his book, *The Science of Getting Rich*, puts it this way: "Everything you see on earth is made from one original substance, out of which all things proceed." That original substance is God.

Let's look at some of God's attributes to help us understand His nature and ability. We'll see ourselves differently if we can grasp His nature and ability. We'll glimpse God's essence and power in us, allowing us to better understand our own:

- God is *eternal*, "...from everlasting to everlasting you are God"— *Psalm 90:2*. He has no beginning and no end. God cannot die; He is immortal.

- God is *infinite*: God has no limits.

- God is *omnipresent*: He is everywhere at once. There's no place where God isn't present.

- God is *omniscient*: God knows everything. He has perfect knowledge of all things past, present, and future.

- God is *omnipotent*: He has unlimited power to do whatever He wants and needs not seek anyone's permission or assistance.

The Source of All   35

Anything He wants to do, He does. Nothing can stop Him or prevent Him from doing what pleases Him. We have His DNA in us. We are able to do things that we never thought possible. It is because of our belief, obedience, and our faith in Him that He is able to impart this nature and ability to us.

- God is *love*: "God is love; and he that dwelleth in love dwelleth in God, and God in him"—*1 John 4:16*. His love is steadfast, and it endures forever. He loves you and wants a relationship with you. He wants to fellowship with you.

- God is *good*, and He is good to all: He looks out for you to do you good. "The LORD is good to all: and his tender mercies are over all his works"—*Psalm 145:9*. He does not discriminate. He makes the sun rise on the evil and on the good, and He sends rain on the just and on the unjust.

- God is *kind*: "…He is kind unto the unthankful and to the evil"— *Luke 6:35*. He has an affectionate disposition to all men. He is supernaturally generous, even when His generosity is not deserved or returned.

- *God is creative*: "In the beginning God created the heaven and the earth"—*Genesis 1:1*. All things were made through him, and without him was not anything made that was made. He is the origin of all creation. He created you in His image, and *you are His masterpiece,* fearfully and wonderfully made. Of all creation, you are the only creation in God's image with the same creative ability because He has also gifted you with skills and talents. You not only look like Him (spiritually speaking), but you can also emulate Him. He created order from chaos and darkness when He created the Heavens and the Earth with words. You too can create something beautiful of your own—peace, joy, victory, abundance or financial prosperity, health, and much more, with the choice of your words.

- God is *beautiful*: "Thine eyes shall see the king in his beauty: they shall behold the land that is very far off"—*Isaiah 33:17*. When

God created anything, the Bible says, He looked at it and said it was good. He loves to see beautiful things and created you wonderfully in His image. His thoughts and creations, including you, are beautiful. He gave us beauty that comes from the inside because through it, we bear His image.

- God is *generous* and provides abundantly: "Now unto him that is able to do exceeding abundantly above all that we ask or think, according to the power that worketh in us"—*Ephesians 3:20*. You cannot have more needs or Desires than He is able to supply. There is more than enough for you, and for everyone, for that matter.

- God is a God of *increase*: "Now he that ministereth seed to the sower both minister bread for your food, and multiply your seed sown, and increase the fruits of your righteousness"—*2 Corinthians 9:10*. The story of the widow in Zarephath is one example of God's ability to bring an *increase* in any situation. There was a terrible famine, and this widow had only one cup of flour and some oil left. She was, to her surprise, visited by a man who told her he was a prophet. He requested some water and a piece of bread for himself. She attempted to argue her case, informing him that there was enough left for her and her son to survive before they starved to death. That wasn't all, though. He instructed her to bake the bread and hand it to him first, which was even more of a test. However, he made a promise on the condition that she carried out his request. As she complied, her flour and oil jars were never empty; her food supply was miraculously extended.

- God is *faithful*: "Let us hold fast the profession of our faith without wavering; (for he is faithful that promised)"—*Hebrews 10:23*. There is no shadow of turning with God. His faithfulness comes down to the Truth that He keeps His promises and stays true to them. He always holds up His end of the deal. He is always looking out for you, and He is reliable. You can count on Him because He is not man that He should lie.

- God is *just*: He shows no partiality and is perfectly just in the way He relates to and treats everyone. He is consistent and always right and just in all His ways.

- God is *Truth*: "Sanctify them through thy truth: thy word is truth"—*John 17:17*. God's Word is God, and if His Word is Truth, then God is Truth. Because He is Truth, He cannot lie. *Hebrews 6:18* states it is impossible for God to lie. You can have confidence, therefore, that everything He has said about you is not a lie; it is Truth! Truth is that which conforms to reality as it is perceived by God. He knows all things extensively and completely, so we can trust anything He says. Truth is not defined by our own subjective standards but determined by the Source of Truth Himself, God. If He has said you are rich, it means you are rich, regardless of what your bank statement shows. If He has said nothing is impossible unto you, it means you can do all things, because He will make it possible. Don't try to use your senses to explain or justify things of the Spirit—the Spirit of God. It follows, therefore, that all these attributes of God are Truth. As long as Earth remains, these Truths will never change because they cannot change; they are Truths.

"So God created man in his own image, in the image of God created he him; male and female created he them"—*Genesis 1:27*. We are further told that He breathed into man, and man became a living soul. He imparted his power to us. It was a combination of Divine elements, spiritual energy, and a physical substance that gave us life and fulfilled His promise to make mankind in His image. Any living thing, unless genetically modified, will give life to its kind or species. You have God's nature and ability if you are created by God.

God's nature is to exult good; His ability is that He can do what He wills. If you are like Him in your nature, you will produce good; if you are like Him in your ability, all things will be possible unto you. If a person is made in the image of God, he has a capacity for all that God possesses and experiences. To know this about yourself is self-awareness. Self-assurance and self-control begin with self-knowledge. If you know that you are like God in your nature, then you will regulate yourself to do only good; if you know that you have God's power, then you will expect to be able to accomplish whatever God says you can do.

The Essence of Life or Purpose

You were created by God for a purpose. You are His handiwork, created to do good works. Life is a gift from God that we should appreciate and enjoy every day. He desires an ongoing relationship with you and has a goal for your life. You were called on to represent His will and nature and His life and Divine qualities that are for your good and the good of others.

The beauty of life is that you are not left alone to attain this goal. God has provided everything necessary for you to succeed in your calling. He knows where, how, and when the blessings will come, so keep your relationship with God close, and take Him at His Word. Remember that He has a plan for you, and it is designed to make your life a tremendous success.

Keep your eyes open for opportunities in which you can serve others using your unique abilities, talents, and personality traits. God's master plan for everyone includes serving others in some way or another during their lifetime. You were created with certain characteristics from the start, which add to your value as an individual.

Keep your heart and Mind open to listen to God's guidance in your life. His will is always best for you. The spiritual dimension of your life includes recognizing the opportunities He places before you so that you can accomplish His plans for your success.

Life is about living, life is a mystery, life isn't always fair, and it has its highs and lows, and so on. When you have the opportunity to inquire about what people think about life, you hear things such as these. Some people believe they are the helpless recipients of whatever life throws at them. If you want to lead a meaningful life, you must break away from the crowd and acquire a different perspective on life. People go to school in order to acquire knowledge. However, no institution can teach you everything there is to know about life, simply because they cannot.

It is usually preferable to utilize a curriculum, or some form of course outline prepared by the subject's or course's author, to educate on a topic or teach a program. When this is done, the learner is more likely to experience the subject matter much more comprehensively and possibly attain the course's objective. In that same context, it makes sense that if we want to live life at the best possible level and manifest the Creator's intention, we will have to follow God's curriculum. To deviate from it is the recipe for a substandard experience of life with no guarantee of attaining or manifesting the Creator's intention or purpose.

You are *not an accident*. "Thine eyes did see my substance, yet being unperfect; and in thy book all my members were written, which in continuance were fashioned, when as yet there was none of them"— *Psalm 139:16*.

You were meticulously planned for. Your arrival in this world was not by accident. Perhaps you were informed that you were an accident. You may have been a mistake to your parents, but you were God's idea. You were already in God's thoughts before your parents entered the picture. *Your life is a Divine arrangement with a special value and purpose.* He knew all there was to know about you and had planned your birth since he had a goal for your life. "For we are his workmanship, created in Christ Jesus unto good works, which God hath before ordained that we should walk in them"—*Ephesians 2:10*.

For many people, life is a mystery. People simply live not knowing what life is all about or what they are supposed to do with this wonderful opportunity of life. Many unanswered questions linger in their minds as they go through the motions every day. Life is not a one-time event; it's a real journey with a purpose. If God is the author of life, He must have a reason for you being here. Knowing Him will give meaning to life and knowing His purpose for you will give your life direction.

World-famous iPhone maker, Apple, is well-known for its outstanding products. Steve Jobs was proud of his team and their creations. "Design isn't just about what it looks and feels like. Design is how it works," he stated. The charger and instructions are included in the box when you buy an iPhone. As an iPhone user, I may be biased, but the same will be true for Samsung, for example. Apple wants its products to work well, and so does your Creator. Without the charger, your iPhone or Samsung battery will last only for so long. God has a purpose for you, and He provides all that is needed for you to function efficiently and effectively. He is *the Great Provider.* "And God is able to make all grace abound toward you; that ye, always having all sufficiency in all things, may abound to every good work"—*2 Corinthians 9:8.*

In the wonderful narrative of creation, there was a lovely garden called Eden. In the garden, everything for a pleasant existence was provided. Man had no needs then because he had all he needed and even a river to enjoy. All he had to do was to maintain creation. Man was to take care of Earth and multiply because He is a God of increase. God intended man to have fellowship with Him for His own pleasure. When God created Adam, he had finished creating everything else, so the world was prepared for him. Adam met God resting from all creation. It is important to note here that everything you need or could ever desire to have, seen or unseen with your physical eyes, already exists in the spiritual realm. Man's existence was meant to be a good, peaceful, and struggle-free life from the beginning. Man was originally in harmony with God until he separated himself from Him.

Many people are confronted with overwhelming financial difficulties as a result of man's refusal to acknowledge his real Source. Some individuals think their supply comes from the government, while others trust in their paychecks from their job, and yet others count on the generosity of friends and relatives. Anything else, other than God, is just a channel. You must center your attention on God rather than the channel. The fact is that God is your Source, and He alone has a blueprint for your existence.

Money is not the only thing that determines your financial success. Money is, nevertheless, an important component of wealth creation and financial well-being. The Truth is that you don't have to be a member of an elite group to achieve financial success. *You are destined to prosper, and riches and abundance are your birthrights.* Your Creator desires the best for you, and this includes financial success. There's nothing wrong with your Desire for money or more money. Your Creator wishes you to have a happy and successful life. To do so, you'll need money to connect your Desires with those who can help you attain them or provide the services you need. If you have a great deal of it, the more you can experience and enjoy the good in creation, and the more you can be a blessing to others. You should not feel guilty about desiring more money. As *Psalm 35:27* says, our Creator, Source, God takes pleasure in our prosperity, and *Deuteronomy 8:18* says He gives us the power to prosper. *Ecclesiastes 10:19* goes on to say that life without money equals to frustration.

"For the eyes of the Lord run to and fro throughout the whole earth, to shew himself strong in the behalf of them whose heart is perfect toward him…"—*2 Chronicles 16:9.* God loves to show His power on your behalf for Earth to know that, indeed, He exists. When you walk in obedience, and your heart stays on Him, He will validate your purpose by causing you to prosper.

All creation is complete; it is finished. On the seventh day God created man and gave him dominion over all creation, and He said to man, go ye and multiply. He rested from all His work. He is done, and it is now up to man to exercise the authority to multiply, as in to increase. The degree of this multiplication is infinite. You must understand your inherent ability to do the same. When a bird pushes its young out of the nest, it expects it to fly. It has its animal instinct to know that the bird is ready to take off and thrive. When God said go ye and multiply, He knew man was ready to take off, so to speak, and excel. Doing so requires mental determination and mental power on your part. This understanding of your ability to create can be called upon at any time it is needed or wanted. Man must understand that the Creator of all things, including man, will not interfere unless He has an absolute reason to, which cannot be disputed. You can create whatever you want to. It is simply up to you to do it.

Understanding the Truth of your origin and purpose is key and fundamental for the manifestation of a lifestyle in which money locates you. Everything that you desire that is in keeping with God's character will be yours. It is He who seeks to express His nature of increase, beauty, love, creativity, and abundance through you. There is no such thing as too much money. Whatever you need to make your Desire come true can never be withheld from you. If it's money, it will find you. If it's a lover, they will find you. If it's a friend, they will come to you. *By seeing yourself differently, with God's ability in you, money will locate you because you'll use money as a means of exchange to create whatever good thing you desire.* Now that you know that you possess this ability to create anything, do not forget the infinite number of possibilities that are available by simply knowing what is possible—*anything.*

Chapter 3 Exercise: Who Do You See in the Mirror? Part 2

With a deeper knowledge of Truth and a more comprehensive awareness of self, go back to that same mirror and take another look with the same eyes that previously gazed into it. Who do you see in the mirror?

Take a few minutes to let the information in this section sink in, and jot down who you think you are now. Remember the cat looking into a mirror in chapter two? The cat sees himself as a lion in the reflection. Do you consider yourself simply as a human being, or do you perceive yourself as a Super Being?

I have been awakened to my true identity. I am the result of Source's creative energy, and I have Source's DNA. The limitless creative power of Source is manifested in and through me in a variety of ways, making me a co-creator. All things are possible for me.

_____

_____

_____

_____

_____

_____

_____

_____

_____

_____

_____

_____

CHAPTER 4

Align Yourself with Source

———— ❧ ————

"Effortless manifestation, your natural modus operandi
when in alignment with Source."

—The author, Joan Ekobena

The invention of the lightbulb is credited to Thomas Edison. Some historians claim that there were over twenty inventors, but Edison's invention made power distribution from a centralized Source economically viable. As important as the lightbulb is to our regular lives, it is useless on its own. To produce light, it requires a good connection to a Source of power. When the connection is bad or unstable, the flow of energy will be interrupted, resulting in reduced brightness and/or flickering light. In terms of our ability to manifest as intended by our Creator, you and I are no different from the lightbulb. To radiate the beauty and excellence of Source, we must be connected to our Source. This connection is referred to here as *alignment*. This profound and powerful alignment demonstrates our oneness with Source. The Law of Divine Oneness states that we are all connected to Source and one another because we all derive our being from Source.

You must maintain a connection with your origin, your Source. Most plants must be connected to the ground in order to grow and produce excellent fruit. Similarly, fish, like all aquatic animals, can't survive outside of water. Your real self, your inner man, came from God and must remain connected to God. Staying connected to God is your assurance of a joyful, successful, and productive life.

One dictionary defines alignment as parts of something that are in the proper position relative to each other. If you're like most people, the first thing that comes to Mind when you hear the word *alignment* is aligning automobile wheels. According to Les Schwab Tire Center, "alignment assures your tires meet the road at the proper angle, your wheels are pointing straight, and your tires are centered in the wheel wells." Wheel alignment aligns the angles of your car's wheels to manufacturer-recommended specifications for optimum gas mileage, optimal road contact, a smooth ride, and maximum tire life. It is easy to understand and see the importance of alignment in this context.

So, how about you being in alignment with Source? What does it mean to be in alignment with Source? It simply means *coming into agreement with Source in your thoughts, beliefs, words, and actions.* As you may recall, everything that exists, including yourself, emanates from Source. Being created in God's image means God projected a portion of Himself forward into physical form or expression. This projection became the physical you, with thinking ability and emotions. You, on the other hand, still have your spiritual self. You now have a clear picture of yourself from both the physical and spiritual (inner man or higher self) standpoints. Only by relating and remaining in oneness, in spirit, can we communicate with God. It is your spirit that must be aligned with Source; therefore, you must first have an understanding of yourself from these two perspectives. In other words, just as car wheels must be aligned to the wheel wells, your spirit must likewise be aligned with God's Spirit to produce excellence and achieve your Desires.

So how will you know if you are in alignment? In order to align yourself with Source, you need to understand what it means to be created in God's image, as I have already described in chapter three. The qualities described in that chapter, while not a complete list, may be used as a benchmark or a guide to determine how well aligned with Source you are. There is oneness with Source in perfect alignment. You are in *a state of consciousness that is inseparable from Source.* His Desires, will, and purpose become your Desires, will, and purpose. Take this as an illustration. When you mix glass B's clear spring water with glass A's clear spring water, there is no visible change; the liquids have become indistinguishable. Both liquids have become one; there is oneness. At that point, the characteristics, qualities, and nature of both liquids are identical; you can't tell which liquid was in glass B or A.

Let us look at another example. When you are in perfect alignment with Source, you are in complete harmony or in sync with Him. Today, many individuals and organizations work with multiple devices such as laptops, tablets, iPads, cell phones, and desktop computers. As they switch between devices, synchronization lets them work in real time on any device they're using at any one moment. On each device, they're able to access the same contacts, messages, and calendar appointments. In this state of congruity, you are reflecting the image of Source. No wonder Apostle Paul said "…as He is, so are we in this world"—*1 John 4:17.*

When you are in harmony with Source, your goals are His Desires that He wants manifested through you. God wants your Desires and His Desires to match; as a result, your intentions will always reflect His vision and purpose for your life. God is continuously increasing and expressing Himself through you by His nature of increase and prosperity. Because of this Truth, you don't need to be concerned about money; it will locate you to accomplish that increase. However, laws govern money and finances, and when we come to be in agreement with these laws, we find ourselves positioned in the flow of God's nature of increase and prosperity.

You can begin to see why it is imperative to be aligned and *remain aligned* with Source. *Alignment to Divine order is a must. Things have to be done in a certain way; refuse to leave things to chance or luck.* There are no limitations when you are connected to the Source of all things visible

Synchronization

and invisible. You may ask why. The reason is that your Desires and ideas are those of Source for whom failure is impossible. He is the origin of all intelligence, information, and comprehension—the origin of all funds, financial or otherwise, required for the fulfillment of any Desire. Even more remarkable is that all that is required for this manifestation will be available with minimal effort. God empowers you and establishes you. He will give you the ability to make your Desires happen. This is because He loves you very much, and when you are in unity with Him, failure is impossible. Do not fall for people who tell you that if it is too easy, it can't be real. If someone tells you this, they are ignorant of the nature of reality itself!

Remember, you are made of your physical and spiritual self. Your spirit, on the other hand, is what becomes aligned with Source. Your physical self, composed of your body and controlled by your senses, cannot align with Source.

Your spirit is linked to Source, communicates with, and is in fellowship with Source when you are in alignment. As a result, the process of thought transference allows ideas to enter your Mind, brain, and body so that you may take action and create reality or manifest your Desire. Manifestation here can be seen as the harvest of the fruits of the union of your spirit and God's Spirit. Consider it this way: When a seed is planted in perfect soil with all the necessary factors, it is certain to yield a generous and bountiful harvest. All of the variables are perfect in Source.

You must realize that, in alignment, Source creates through you; you become a *conduit*. You are the perfect vessel for God to express His beauty, majesty, strength, expansion, and abundance. This expression happens through manifestation. It pleases Him to see only good things happen in and through your life because others will see your good works and glorify your Father in heaven. God is far more concerned about your health and success than you may think. He is all about growth, and He expects us to grow and multiply. "And you, be ye fruitful, and multiply; bring forth abundantly in the earth, and multiply therein"—*Genesis 9:7.*

This is how the manifestation of money works: Money comes to you as a result of you being a conduit for good things. You have a clear vision and a positive mindset. When you think about that which you desire, do so in the following manner: Let your thoughts be those of an expanding Universe. Think big—don't limit what the Creator can do through your life! Money is simply energy. It has no boundaries or limitations on where or when it can occur. In other words, there are no laws against money manifesting itself into anyone's life! Of course, we must follow certain principles, but these principles are simple once they're known and understood.

Many people talk about how difficult it is for them to see the abundance all around them because their focus is on the limiting thoughts of lack that are almost engulfing them. They cannot even begin to see themselves as a channel for Source.

I am asking you now: Are your thoughts expanding or contracting? When you think of money, do you feel tightness in your body, constriction around your throat and forehead? If so, then stop dwelling on limiting thoughts, such as where or when money can manifest itself in your life; instead, focus on an abundant Universe—on expansion. Place yourself inside an expansive Universe by thinking big picture—millions of dollars coming into your life instead of mere thousands.

The Law of Attraction is always working—it's a universal law that requires no upkeep, no maintenance. It is perfectly natural for Source to express Himself through you by giving you more money! You've been given everything you need to live a rich and abundant life. God has provided a conduit for abundance to flow into your life. The Source I speak of is none other than the Spirit of the Creator Himself, who resides within each one of us. Your job now is simply to align your thoughts with this stream of abundance that wishes to come through the vehicle that is your body every minute of every day. The good news is you are not alone in this process; help can be found everywhere if you are open enough to become aware of it.

Source wants you to reveal His nature to the world around you, and you are His collaborator and co-creator. You must believe this Truth. Can you begin to imagine the things you might co-create with the Source of Infinite Intelligence and Supernatural Ability?

Acquiring money and the ability to do more is not some strange idea separate from the nature of God, but rather an expression of Source. You were born with unlimited potential—power over anything that exists. This includes the power to create more money, which everyone does through their beliefs about what money can be used for and how much they will receive.

Through you, He accomplishes His purposes in limitless ways and does the same with everyone who is connected to Him.

Believing is seeing, and when you see yourself as a powerful creator of your reality—by using your Mind and the skills that come to you for this purpose, then you will create more money.

Money is a symbol of God in action in and through you. And when people see you in your world, they will know that you are connected to the Power Source of the Universe, Infinite Intelligence, and Supernatural Ability, because money flows through your life effortlessly, unless you block it with fear or judgmental thinking.

If you have blocked money from your life, then by changing how you think about what money means to you—what it is used for and how much of it is good enough for you—then money can be yours once again.

Money locates you in the world because it belongs to you. It reflects the world of unlimited possibilities, infinite choices, and total freedom. You don't have to be concerned about your ideas or resources becoming depleted by others. If you find yourself in this position, a competitive mentality may begin to seep in. There is no rivalry or competition with Source. He is God in and of Himself.

You can create infinite abundance for yourself by connecting to the energy Source of life and Intelligence, God. You actually co-create with God when you receive beautiful things in your life, such as money or love or health or inspiration. And this process must be allowed so that God may do His work in bringing everything good into and through your life. Then there is no limit to how much money can come into your life because it has come from Him through you.

The Source of all things is with you in everything that exists. And He works through you to accomplish His purposes throughout eternity. Because Source is infinite, your Mind is infinite and so are your resources for achieving anything you want—including money!

As an employer, one of my goals is to meet or exceed a certain number of service hours each month. To accomplish this, the marketing representatives must participate in marketing efforts and activities that lead to new business. Because we want to reach our goals, we give them the tools they need to do their job effectively and succeed. They are given a cell phone, a business credit card, company clothing, and a corporate automobile as well as marketing materials. How much more of God's resources would He provide to enable His plans to be fulfilled? He will provide abundantly more than enough when we trust Him and focus on aligning ourselves with Him.

So, when you consider doing something that is in line with God's will, just stay aligned with Him, and everything will sooner or later come together for its fulfillment. When money is needed, money will locate you. When the right people need to be in your life, they will. When you're meant to receive a car or something else, it'll happen. God's resources are unlimited and inexhaustible. By giving Him the reins and following His lead, we allow Him to fulfill our every Desire with ease and grace. He has freely supplied you with all you need to serve Him efficiently and successfully. He is a God of excellence and perfection. "And we know that all things work together for good to them that love God, to them who are the called according to his purpose"—*Romans 8:28.*

For two to work together, they must be in agreement. It is no different with Source. *Prepare your spirit to be in agreement with Source.*

"Finally, believers, whatever is true, whatever is honorable and worthy of respect, whatever is right and confirmed by God's word, whatever is pure and wholesome, whatever is lovely and brings peace, whatever is admirable and of good repute; if there is any excellence, if there is anything worthy of praise, think continually on these things [center your Mind on them, and implant them in your heart]. The things which you have learned and received and heard and seen in me, practice these things [in daily life], and the God [who is the Source] of peace and well-being will be with you"—*Philippians 4:8–9 (The Amplified Bible).*

Do not accommodate wrong thoughts; focus on the right thoughts. If you meditate on the wrong thoughts, you worry, and worry produces the wrong results. You get out of alignment or the right frequency when you worry. Rick Warren, in *The Purpose Driven Life,* says, "When God is at the center of your life, you worship, when He is not, you worry."

As you learn to bring your thoughts into obedience with the Law of the Word, hatred, anger, bitterness, unforgiveness and anything that is not consistent with Source will check out, bringing you back into alignment.

Remember the elementary school science experiment with water and oil? Oil and water do not mix well because they have incompatible chemical compositions. When you mix them, they separate over time because one or both of them is trying to find their balance in the mix. Oil molecules will be attracted to other oil molecules, and water molecules to other water molecules. You will align with Source only when you embrace and reflect His nature, as discussed in chapter three. To improve upon this experiment, add liquid soap to the oil and water mixture, and the two liquids will become inseparable. So too, by utilizing God's Word, we may create the right conditions for alignment with Source. When you align your thoughts with Source's principles, money locates you wherever you go because it is drawn to you, much like a piece of metal is drawn to a magnet.

If a lightbulb is connected to a power source, it does not struggle to shine, unless it is faulty or there is a problem with the connection. You have the power to create any wonderful thing you desire, and with less effort, once you have an understanding of God's nature and are connected to Source! We may not be able to live apart from Source, as we are all a part of creation. We must therefore maintain a solid connection with Source if we want to enjoy the riches and abundance available through Source. This is the state in which all of your Desires are fulfilled effortlessly. However, you must first accept this Truth! After you've accepted it, you must then start applying the ideas I've shared with you here. The preceding illustration of a lightbulb might serve as a helpful reminder of this connection.

You are a channel for abundance to the rest of the world. The Creator's purpose is realized when you serve as a channel for His glory. You become a channel for permanent growth and prosperity if you stick to the principles of the Word and remain in harmony with Source.

Because your thoughts are in step with God's goal, you accomplish everything with minimum or no effort. Your life becomes a reflection of abundance with just as much effort as it takes to stay where you are in life now.

Sometimes people align themselves by first seeking knowledge about others' opinions on how they should live their lives. Aligning with the opinions of others aligns us with their Desire and ambition. Doing so breaks our connection to aligning with Source.

Our overriding goal should be to align with our Source, God. Without any doubt, aligning yourself with God brings you prosperity and financial freedom. This aligning begins by being in the right place. For you, that place is where your heart is pointing at all times. The minute you follow your heart's direction toward aligning with the Source of All, money follows. You are aligning yourself with the power that has created all things, and this alignment brings you what you desire. Money will align itself because it seeks its master. It will align itself with you without prejudice, because money isn't aimed at discriminating against people who are poor or rich. Neither does it discriminate by race; it simply wants to find people whose hearts are aligned with the Desires of Source.

We've identified negative beliefs or limiting paradigms, gotten to know our origin, and accepted our origin, our real identity, and our purpose as co-creators with the Source of All. We've also come to understand the significance of being in alignment with our Source. The culmination of aligning with the essence of God as one who continuously seeks to manifest abundance and prosperity through us is the alignment with our unlimited potential. For money to locate you, you must first come to terms with the concepts covered in these chapters in part one. Your success is founded on your acceptance and belief in them.

The groundwork for part two of this book has now been laid. As you go into part two, keep the Truths you've learned in the forefront of your Mind. They'll help you make sense of and easily put into practice the ideas discussed in the following chapters for an effortless manifestation of money in your life.

Chapter 4 Exercise: Align Yourself with Source

What does being in alignment with Source mean to you?

_____

_____

_____

_____

_____

_____

_____

_____

_____

_____

_____

_____

_____

_____

_____

_____

_____

_____

_____

_____

_____

_____

_____

PART 2

CHAPTER 5

Desire

———— ❧ ————

"Desire is possibility seeking expression."

—Ralph Waldo Emerson

The moment you place your focus on what you Desire, that Desire finds its location in the field of infinite possibilities. Desire is possibility seeking expression through you. Desire always seeks an increase, but it does so without denying anything or anyone their needed contribution.

"The starting point of all achievement is desire. Keep this constantly in mind. Weak desires bring weak results just like a small amount of fire makes a small amount of heat."—*Napoleon Hill*

Desire is defined as a compelling feeling that motivates you to achieve or obtain something.

Desire really just means that there is something in you which wants to be manifested, which wants to be expressed. Desire is not only "a Desire" (an idea or thought), but is also always proactive and speaks into existence new possibilities. Desire is the Desire to do, Desire *to build*, Desire to create. Desire is like a child knocking on the door of your life, asking to be born through you. Having a definite Desire is very important because this gives you a starting point to begin manifestation; it puts you in motion, into action. These actions will assist in mobilizing the forces that carry out all manifestations into reality. If you want to get results, you must do something to get them. If you don't take the necessary actions, the golden opportunity (possibility seeking expression) to manifest may pass by; then all that was desired will disappear into oblivion.

Money is a means of exchange, a tool to achieve your ultimate goal. What propels you to act, whether it's toward a specific goal or simply for enjoyment, is Desire. What is your Desire? Or what would you love, as Peggy McColl would say? Perhaps you have a burning Desire in your heart to become someone or do something for yourself or others. Do you want to become the mayor of your city, a Nobel Peace Prize winner, or Ms. Universe? Do you want to adopt a child, sponsor an orphanage, own a jet, start a summer camp program for blind children, travel the world, or be able to afford a certain lifestyle? What would you love? Most of what you want will require money in one form or another. Money is not a goal in and of itself; rather, it's a tool that can be used to achieve your Desire. Even if it's just kept in your bank account and makes your bank statement look good, it gives you a feeling of financial security that may be satisfying. Even if you want to create one million or one billion dollars, your real Desire may be the sense of security and calm you feel from knowing that you have all of that money, financial stability, and are debt-free. Desire does not distinguish between large and small. It does not judge your intention as to whether something is too small or excessive, but rather pushes all things equally to be manifested.

Money locates you as a means to an end—your Desire. When you feel the energy of Desire for something, it may seem as if it has arisen out of nowhere, but there was always some sort of groundwork being laid for its manifestation before you were consciously aware of having the Desire in the first place. *Desire is the seed that becomes your reality.* When the Desire arises in your awareness and you're not ready to accept its fulfillment, then you struggle with the Desire—you want it but don't want it at the same time, depending on your perspective.

Money is abundant in the Universe and will go where it is invited and welcomed. Money will come to you if you have a need or Desire, and it will arrive for you to fulfill or help you realize that Desire.

The one who establishes a Desire has taken the first step toward its manifestation. "Ask, and it shall be given you; seek, and ye shall find; knock, and it shall be opened unto you: For every one that asketh receiveth; and he that seeketh findeth; and to him that knocketh it shall be opened"—*Matthew 7:7–8*. "But my God shall supply all your need according to his riches in glory by Christ Jesus"—*Philippians 4:19*.

So, you have this Desire to bring something into existence, such as a luxury resort on a private island for destination weddings. Have you ever paused to consider how this Desire came about? It's not enough to know that God is infinite; you must appreciate the limitless possibilities He offers you. What do you think the Mind of infinite possibilities is capable of?

Source is constantly revealing Himself, expanding with additional Sources of supply for you, and making it possible for you to have more than you could hope for or desire, no matter where your life takes you or what happens in it. Source is the same today as yesterday and will remain so tomorrow. His infinite resources are there for you, and always there for anyone who has a Desire to draw from them, no matter how unrealistic their Desires may seem to others.

When you are aligned with Source, His Desires will come to you as your own. That's when some may say they had a vision or a dream to do this or that. Some have even said while meditating or praying that they heard a voice tell them to do something. When we follow the guidance we receive, it leads us to our Desires. If that was your experience, you may have been aligned with Source.

When this happens, your passion will be so strong and all-consuming that you'll have no choice but to accept it. That Desire would have come through *Divine Inspiration*. If you have an idea or thought of what you Desire when in alignment with Source, it means Source has put this possibility out there in the Universe and is now asking for your attention and participation in it becoming real. It comes pre-loaded with all of the components, connections, and other resources needed to create it. We could say that this Desire is spiritual energy that exists in us and simply wishes to take a tangible form. As it expresses itself through us, we can begin to create the experiences that Desire is expressing. That is when you do the impossible with the least effort. Whatever that Desire is, money will locate you for its manifestation because God's Desire must be accomplished. You'll have to be careful not to get in the way by allowing your success blockers, such as limiting paradigms or negative beliefs, to take over. We'll identify more success blockers in the following chapters.

On the other hand, you may not be sure if your Desire came through Divine Inspiration. It might be the result of your own thoughts or ideas. For example, you could remark, "It just occurred to me to do this," or "This is something I would want to achieve," or "I would just love to have a million dollars in my bank account." If this is the case, your Desire must possess certain qualities, which I refer to as *manifestation attributes*. The more of these attributes your Desire has, the more likely it is to come true. When a Desire contains all of these qualities, it becomes manifest. If some are lacking, you will either experience a delayed manifestation or no manifestation at all.

Using the example of the Desire to visit a luxury resort, you might have been inspired by a National Geographic or travel program on television. That is great! It is a typical human inclination to want to accomplish more, be more, or desire more. Desire is our natural state of being, an innate part of our nature. We don't necessarily desire because we are greedy or just want to consume things. These ideas have more to do with the Desire for accomplishment, Desire for contribution, Desire for joy, Desire to help others. Desire is the basis of all our great accomplishments. Any living thing is either increasing, or it is decreasing to its death. In living, there's a natural Desire to increase to a fuller expression of oneself. Even the process of thinking leads to more thoughts and more thinking, and one action leads to another.

What would you love? *You must state what you desire.* The Bible instructs us to state our Desires, ask for what we want, and it will be given to us. You must state what you Desire to receive. On His way to Jerusalem, Jesus encountered a blind beggar named Bartimaeus. He cried out for mercy, but Jesus asked him what he wanted. Of course, Jesus knew what Bartimaeus wanted, but he asked him to state it. He responded that he wanted to see. Writing what you desire is essential, but stating it aloud activates and impresses it on your Subconscious Mind. Putting it out to the Universe implies a certain degree of confidence that it will come true.

To say what you don't want is a waste of time and effort. All your Desires should be stated in positive terminology. For example, instead of saying, "I want to be debt-free," instead say, in your Mind, or with full conviction in a self-determined manner, something such as, "My money currently is," and give the correct figure. Instead of saying, "I want to lose weight," say in your Mind or state with full conviction in a self-determined manner something such as, "My weight currently is," and give the correct figure. This is more likely to produce the desired effect.

How clear is your Desire? Once you have stated what your Desire is; you must have complete clarity about it for it to be realized. If you don't know where you are going, you'll never get there. Saying you want a new home is not enough. Be as precise and as detailed as possible. This reminds me of the meticulous detail and precise directions that God gave the Israelites when they constructed the tabernacle. Give your Subconscious Mind something to work with that isn't vague.

Take the time to make a detailed description of what you would like your Desire to look or feel like when realized in the physical. Remember, everything was formed in the spiritual realm, and all you have to do now is bring your Desires into reality. Let's go with the example of a beautiful new home. If you want to manifest money for a new home, be specific. What size? Square footage? Number of bedrooms and bathrooms? You get the idea. The more detailed the picture is in your Mind, the better. Is it relatively new or brand-new? What color is the wood floor or marble floor? Can you imagine yourself giving a friend a tour of your new home? Can you see yourself lounging by the infinity pool with visitors? What does it feel like to be in your beautiful new home? When that happens, the Desire for a home, which you previously thought was only a dream, becomes real to you as if it already exists here and now. I suppose I was drawn to using this example since I love real estate, and having a beautiful new home is one of my top Desires. It is on my goal card and visualization board, which I will explain later. I have a mental image of the floor plan and can quickly go through it in my head. I've driven past the site where this house will be constructed and know how to get there, even without a GPS.

If you're manifesting a new car, get clear about the make, model, color, and features. If you're asking for a raise at work, be specific about how much you'd like to see in your paycheck.

How strong or compelling is your Desire? Your Desire must be very intense in your Mind to the point that it is palpable in your body. Desire that is so strong, it's like a burning fire shut up in your bones—unquenchable Desire; you can't stop thinking about it. It whirls up in you a feeling of urgency. Circumstances have no bearing on this unstoppable Desire. Your Desire must be strong enough that your focus doesn't waver. It takes over your Mind and your thoughts. It's unshakable, and you can't shove it aside; it takes over. This type of Desire is fearless, entertaining no impossibilities. You care about your Desire and put forth your utmost effort to make it a reality. You must be passionate about it to the point of laughing at any impossibilities. A Desire is a wish for something you would love to have but you have no complete understanding of how it will become a reality. It must be so grand that the thought of it almost scares you. Make it as big as you can, to the point that you are forced to attribute its success to God or Source. Desire is just a thought until you bring it into existence with your thoughts and actions. If you don't know how, that shouldn't keep you from wanting anything wonderful. Feel confident in your decision, and let God decide how and when it will be realized.

When your Desire is strong enough, it attracts money like a magnet. The Mind-Body connection is so powerful when balanced correctly; if you feel something deep in your Mind without any resistance toward its manifestation (which comes from fear), then all of a sudden there can be an overflow of energy surrounding this thing. When God is ready to deliver it, money will be coming at you from many directions.

I'd like to add a word of caution here that will be addressed in a subsequent chapter. Manifesting a Desire will entail some effort or action on your part. Desire makes you do; it makes you take action.

Desire should be proportionate to your ability to execute it. For instance, if you have a Desire to soar like an eagle, you will not be able to manifest this Desire if you don't have wings. Desire that is *realistic* will find expression in your life. You must be able to execute your Desire through action for it to become reality. Desire that is *unrealistic* will produce no manifestation or a much-delayed one.

Prepare to endure rigorous training exercises if you want to break Michael Jordan's basketball title record. Just because you desire something does not mean you will manifest it. Whatever it is you want to manifest, your Desire drives you to take action in order for the thing you desire to happen. According to Joseph Murphy, "Desire is the power behind all action. Desire pushes man; it is the goal of action." For some, visualizing a Desire and everything else covered in prior sections is all they believe it takes to bring their wish into reality. If that were the case, many would be able to realize their Desires. More action is required, and your passion offers you the motivation and power to carry out what needs to be done in order for it to happen. You must be able to participate in any action that is required for your wish to come true. In the example of Michael Jordan, you must be able to jump, and jump very high.

What is the motive behind your Desire?

You must have the right motive. We've already seen that your motivation must be in alignment with Source. It must be for the purpose of doing good for yourself and/or others in order to improve them or bring some form of increase in their lives. Is it that you want to be better than someone else? Is there a concern of scarcity that others will get to it first, and there won't be enough for you? Such a motivation stems from egoism, rivalry, and the dread of scarcity. The Universe is abundant in every area. Source increases you and yet does not take from another to satisfy your Desire. You might be at the same frequency of that which you desire, as required, but you won't be aligned with Source. Supreme Intelligence examines the heart and Mind of a person, which is why you should be very careful about your intentions. You must be in tune with the infinite flow of universal energy and conscious of God's will for your highest good. You must have the right motive to be successful in your manifestations. The motive must come from a place of love, abundance, service to others, etc. All wrong motives will lead to failure.

Consider how, when the children of Jacob decided to be like their neighbors, they asked God for a King, even though Samuel advised them against it. Well, Samuel was commissioned to go anoint their new King from the house of Jesse. Upon his arrival, he saw one of Jesse's sons, Eliab, a tall and handsome man. He thought, surely, that must be him. But God said, hold on, not so quickly. He said, "But the Lord said unto Samuel, Look not on his countenance, or on the height of his stature; because I have refused him: for the Lord seeth not as man seeth; for man looketh on the outward appearance, but the Lord looketh on the heart"—*1 Samuel 16:7*. What is the motive behind your Desire? Is it pride or covetousness?

You must focus on your Desire. Many, including myself, have multiple Desires. It is possible to manifest more than one Desire at a time. For example, you may have one major Desire that when fulfilled takes care of many others. However, I personally have found it more practical to focus on one Desire at a time. This is especially true when it comes to visualization. You can then devote your full attention and energy to that particular Desire. The more you keep the vision, right emotions, and feeling, the better. In doing so, you continuously impress them on your Subconscious Mind as you make a mental image of them.

How you feel about your Desire will also influence how much attention you pay to it. You must feel good about the Desire. The more positive your feelings are and the more excited you are about what you'll do with the money, the simpler it will be to manifest it. You cannot manifest a million dollars while thinking of how broke you are. It is essential that your emotion matches the Desire, and it's necessary to make sure you feel good about what you see in your Mind's eye.

You concentrate on your goal by repeating positive affirmations about it every day, looking at your goal card and visualization board frequently. However, you should not be so absorbed and preoccupied with your Desire that God, the Source of it, becomes relegated to the back burner.

The future becomes the present. To many, this is an intriguing yet perplexing idea. How can your future goal become a reality now? The answer is simple: The location of your future goal is inside your Mind. The idea of how fantastic it will be once you acquire that thing, achieve that goal, or realize your Desire fills you with excitement. Manifesting what you want into the present moment puts you in a position to get it. The common adage, "Fake it until you make it," seems appropriate here. You must imagine and feel as if you currently have what you would love. To be able to manifest your Desires, you must first imagine yourself as the person you want to be, or imagine you have all the money you desire, or feel that you are living in your ideal home, or leading the life you've always wanted. When you bring the future into the present, you are, in effect, confirming that it is possible and real. You must maintain that feeling with your willpower and faith, knowing that it has already been accomplished. You will continue to be in your present financial condition if you continue to perceive yourself as one who is broke and do not believe and feel that you are wealthy. You must first envision yourself as the future individual you want to be in order to evolve. As Neville Goddard said, "You must imagine that you are already experiencing what you Desire." This idea is based on the Law of Assumption, which is a method of manifesting your Desires by having a state of Mind, feelings, and belief that your Desire has already been fulfilled. According to Neville Goddard, it's not mere action but also your state of Mind that will result in the manifestation of your Desire. When you get up in the morning, can you picture yourself waking up in your lovely new mansion's luxurious master bedroom suite? Do you detect the exquisite floral fragrance from your well-maintained garden's meticulously trimmed flowers? Your feelings have a significant impact on the manifestation of any Desire. *Ensure that you're continuously seeing your Desire in the present and appreciating the emotions associated with it as if it has already been accomplished.* Speak of it as if it is presently here and you are living or enjoying it now. When you talk about your Desire in the future tense, you are confirming that it does not exist or is absent, and you don't want to communicate such messages to your Subconscious Mind. When thinking or talking about your Desire, preface your sentences with "I am so happy, I am so grateful, I am very excited, or I feel so great now that…"

The Desire must be noble and bring about a positive result and *increase* when it is accomplished. Consider this question: Is the Desire beneficial to me, that is, my body, Mind, and spirit? Is it also beneficial to others? According to Wallace Wattles, "Increase is what all men and all women are seeking. It is the urge of Infinite Intelligence within them seeking fuller expression." God is all for increase, and He wants the same for you. After creating man, He said, "…go ye and multiply." As you increase, you are expressing His ever-increasing glory, you are better able to help others, and everyone increases and has a better experience of life and creation. So, your Desire must be one that when realized, brings good and increase to others as well as yourself. It must increase the good in life, not take away from it. God loves increase. As you increase others, Infinite Intelligence will make things fall in place for your continuous increase. This is best illustrated by the idea of the Impression of Increase, which states that anyone who has an encounter with you leaves feeling better or improved than before they met you. It's all about creating a positive impact on the people we meet.

Dare to dream big! How big is your Desire? Dream of something that seems impossible or unattainable. Once identified, believe in the dream with all your heart. Many people, including myself, have been overly cautious in our expectations. This behavior may be attributed to paradigms or a lack of belief in one's ability to achieve one's intended goal. Many analytical minds share this experience. My husband and I run a home care company, so like many business owners, we generally sit down toward the end of each year to set goals for the next year. He's usually fast in coming up with the revenue objective for the next year. My initial reaction is usually, "How is that possible in light of the current situation?" I'd start by listing several reasons why that revenue objective was out of reach. It surprises me that, between the two of us, I am more vocal about my faith and how everything is feasible with God. However, when it comes to something as important as this, I put my thinking hat on, and my analytical Mind kicks in. As a numbers person, I crunched the numbers in order to come up with what I thought was more realistic—sad. The reality is that I've generally ended up with an annual revenue that was not far from my expectations. I was relying on my own limited ability. In hindsight, my husband may have been applying this idea (dare to dream big) while I was relying on our own abilities and skills. I'm curious what it would have been like if both of us had agreed to aim higher. As I became aware of the power of having the appropriate qualities for any Desire, my thinking has evolved. One year, I went along with him, dreaming big, and it paid off. Under all of the circumstances I'd previously stated to justify my more "realistic" perspective, we exceeded our revenue expectations. I'm more aware now, and I see things differently. According to Ralph Waldo Emerson, "The Mind, once stretched by a new idea, never returns to its original dimensions." You're reading this book, and I have a strong feeling that you want to do more in your life or develop in some area, so don't be afraid to aim high. Don't limit yourself; dream big.

God is the Source of all and operates in grandeur. He is the God of Unequaled Greatness. He has provided us with a tool, our Mind, which allows us to think big and co-create magnificent and spectacular things. Don't limit God by thinking small. Use your Mind to stretch your imagination and your Desire. Once you come to the realization that you will be unable to accomplish it on your own, and that this Desire must take form in the material world, you have entered God's domain, His energy Source, thus creating energy to make things happen. That is where God comes into play and you start to have faith in Him to make it happen, but this happens as a result of your adherence to His principles and laws in this book. These principles and laws are based on His unchanging and unfailing nature. Don't fall into the trap of feeling guilty for wanting too much. That's a mindset that has to be changed. There is more supply for every good Desire. There are no limits in the world of possibilities; the only thing that matters is your creativity. What He did for someone, He'll do for you in the same scenario. So, dare to dream big.

Desire must be empowered by faith. Desire, when accompanied by fear, becomes like a seed thrown onto hard rock, and Desire, when backed by faith, becomes like a seed thrown on fertile soil where it can grow infinitely. Desire, when it has a desired effect upon your Subconscious Mind and creates a sense of certainty in your Mind about its fulfillment, will manifest. Desire strengthened by confidence is Desire manifested—not confidence in oneself, but confidence in the Source of All, God.

A Desire that is both clear and passionate in its fulfillment, as well as being backed by faith, is similar to a seed that has been cultivated with effort and then allowed to germinate, develop, and produce fruit. You then allow Source to determine the how in spite of what appears on the surface. You are not moved by what you see or what your senses bring back to you. You trust that in due time your Desire will manifest into reality because God works through His law, and His law never fails.

Chapter 5 Exercise: The Dream Big Challenge—What Would You Love?

Some people already have their Desires at their fingertips ready to jot down. They know exactly what they want. Some may have to think about it and then really think about it. If you are part of the latter group, no worries! Feel free to use the widest stretch of your imagination and/or prayerfully think of what you would love. Dare to dream and dream big. Let yourself drift away into the land of so-called impossibilities, and make a mental image of all you see and feel. As the Desires come to your Conscious Mind, write them down. Don't worry about prioritizing; just let them flow.

_____

_____

_____

_____

_____

_____

_____

_____

_____

_____

_____

_____

_____

_____

CHAPTER 6

You Attract What You Vibrate

———— ❧ ————

"No one can deny you or grant you anything. It all
comes to you by virtue of your vibration."

—*Esther Hicks*

You could have been drawn to this book because you want more money in your life. Like many others, you may be curious and interested in learning how money locates you. You may be the reader who has always imagined money floating in the air and moving toward you, as if you had become a money magnet. Well, in as much as you may not see dollar notes floating toward you, money does have energy, and it, like everything else, vibrates. Money has its own vibrational pattern, so you must shift your perception about money in order to shift your experience with it. This isn't just emotional conditioning, but rather a shift in awareness. Shift into that space where money already is, outside of you, and you will get more of it. Money is a frequency inherent in the Universe, so let's turn up our vibration to match it.

The Law of Vibration

Without getting into quantum physics, we'll discuss the Law of Attraction, the Law of Vibration, and the role of your feelings in attracting money into your life. The Law of Vibration, while not as well-known as the Law of Attraction, is nonetheless the foundation or basis for the Law of Attraction. To take advantage of the Law of Attraction, you must first establish vibrational alignment. The Law of Vibration is based on the concept that everything is energy, and everything moves or vibrates at a certain frequency. Albert Einstein's famous formula, $E=mc^2$, explains the concept of energy: There is no difference between energy and mass. Everything is simply one form of another. Water, ice, and steam are good examples of this. All three states are essentially the same substance. The idea that everything is energy and vibrates similarly applies to both things and people. This vibration is produced by our thoughts, emotions, and feelings, all of which are rooted in our beliefs. Thoughts and emotions, when you consider and feel them, radiate outward, giving off vibrations. Beliefs form the foundation for our thoughts and emotions. They are the basis of who we are, what we think, and how we feel. Once you begin to understand this concept, you can begin to see how it is possible for your feelings about money to either bring more of it into your life or keep it away from you. You may not realize this since you don't perceive it with your physical eyes or comprehend it. Just believe it. For example, because you can't see it, except with the aid of a microscope, you may not believe that your skin is a zoo of germs. It is, however, a Fact that you have about 1.8 m^2 of skin, and more than 1.5 trillion bacteria live on it. Your vibration does not just vanish into thin air; it is not lost or abandoned. The Universe takes in your energy through your vibration; then it is received, processed, and returned to you. Vibrations attract similar thoughts or thought energy and frequencies. Even though you can't see or interact with it, you and others may sense, feel, and react to energy in a conscious or subconscious manner. Have you ever entered a room full of people and felt strangely out of place? The energy in the space is most likely to blame. You may have even reacted by leaving the room. There was a disconnect because the frequency of your energy and that in the space were not in sync or at the same level.

Your brain, like anything else, has energy. Some of that energy is consumed while you think. Your brain produces waves in various frequencies as a result of this activity. These frequencies control your emotions or state of Mind. If you could see these waves, they would look like little squiggles or jagged lines on an EEG monitor. If your brain waves are strong enough to reach out, they will attract similar frequencies from the Universe. It's as if your brain waves are a radio tower. When the frequencies produced by your brain are in line with what you desire to attract in your life, there is vibrational alignment. But how does this happen?

Focus is how. When you concentrate on an object or a desired result, you bring all of your attention to it. While you're doing that, you're re-creating every aspect of the thing or event in your thoughts. Your brain inadvertently starts generating frequencies that resemble the frequency you'd be at if you already had the item in your hands or had already obtained the desired result. In other words, it begins to resonate and get in tune or in harmony with the frequency of that object or desired outcome. We have already established that everything, including our thoughts, have energy. According to the Law of Perpetual Transmutation of Energy, that energy is always moving and changing (almost as if metamorphosed) from one form into another. The energy from our thoughts flowing into our consciousness is transformed into whatever we like by focusing on it.

Vibrational Frequencies

RAISE YOUR VIBRATION TO MATCH THE
VIBRATION OF YOUR DESIRE

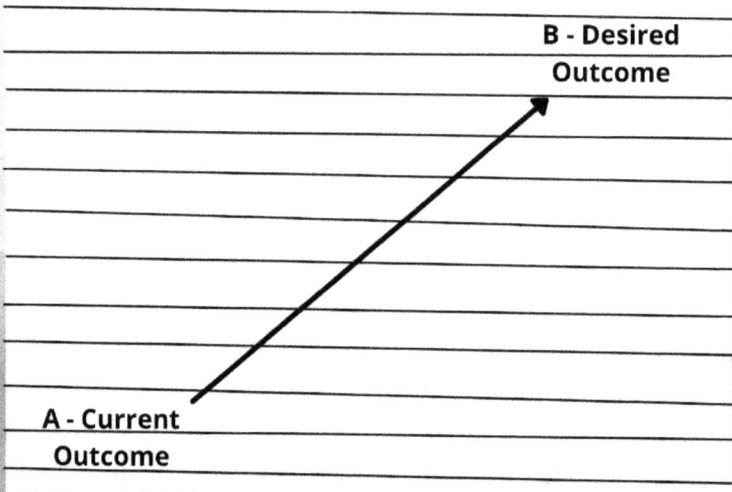

**B - Desired
Outcome**

**A - Current
Outcome**

Raise your vibration

The Law of Attraction

The Law of Vibration is the beginning of the Law of Attraction. The Law of Attraction states that like energy attracts like energy. Your thoughts have energy. If you focus your attention on positive thoughts, such as abundance, love, joy, happiness, and well-being, then your vibration becomes positive. Your thoughts are energy that vibrate to attract similar vibrations. Those who tune in to the frequency of abundance often find it easier to overcome their lack mentality and begin to manifest abundance in their lives quickly. If you think about something, you will start feeling it. You can use this law by simply imagining how you want things to be or using your imagination to create what you want. If it is just one or two things, then that's okay, too! You can use this powerful law to overcome your money blocks and begin to manifest more money into your life. Let me explain this further with an example: You are now attracting things into your life because of what you have been thinking up to this point. If you continue to think about what is bad, your life will always be filled with bad things and missed opportunities. This is because whatever you give your attention to grows and expands in your life. So, if your thoughts about money are that it is hard to get and you do not have any, then how will you ever attract or manifest money into your life by focusing on the bad and giving time and energy to those thoughts?

Like the Law of Gravity, the Law of Attraction works irrespective of your awareness or belief in it; it is law! *You attract into your life what you vibrate.* In essence, you will attract only vibrations that align with your vibrations. Now, remember that everything is energy and vibrates, including your thoughts. So, if you want more money in your life, you cannot have thoughts that hold vibrations of need or lack. What that will do is attract vibrations of need, lack, or poverty. Like energy attracts like energy.

You could be asking, "How do these seemingly scientific ideas relate to aligning oneself with Source?" Let's find out. "For as he thinketh in his heart, so is he"—*Proverbs 23:7.* Your thoughts really matter because they form the basis of who you become. Your life is a manifestation of your thoughts. You create your own reality by the thoughts you choose to focus on. You need to shift your focus from what is wrong or lacking (deficit) to what is right (surplus) in life. Instead of focusing on lack or poverty, start focusing on abundance. Instead of thinking about how you do not have enough money, you should be thinking about how you can make more or attract money into your life.

If you are already in the habit of thinking about lack, poverty, not enough, or scarcity all the time, do not worry! You now have the opportunity to be aware of this law and begin to change your thinking. The moment you become aware and start applying it, then the law will start working on changing your life into what you want it to be.

You must hold an emotionally positive thought or belief in order to be aligned with Source. This emotionally constructive idea or belief vibrates at a frequency that is in harmony with the emotions expressed in God's nature. What exactly do I mean? In chapter three, you read about some of the characteristics of God's nature. Love is the most important of them all. God is love personified.

"God is love; and he that dwelleth in love dwelleth in God, and God in him"—*1 John 4:16.*

When you like someone or something, you may feel good emotions or sentiments that create high frequencies. It's all summed up in the scripture quotation above. You vibrate at a high frequency when you love or live in love, and you attract vibrations of that intensity. God, who is Love and the Source of All, is at a high frequency level. At this level, you are in harmony with Source. This is where your vibrations must be in order to attract anything and everything, including money, from Source.

Take, for example, trying to listen to the news on a radio station. If you want to listen to the news, you must first tune in to the radio station broadcasting it. The radio waves that come out of the radio towers carry certain information depending on the frequency and strength of those signals. Your thoughts and resulting brain waves produce energy much like a radio station does.

We had a little AM/FM shortwave radio as a child, and it was a real treasure since we didn't have a television. We had to pull out the antenna, adjust it at various angles, or move the radio to another location in our home in order to receive a stronger signal. We still had to manually turn the dial until we got the signal for that station, no matter how good or poor the reception was. In other words, we had to adjust the radio dial to the correct station in order to hear and listen to the news or other programs.

It's also the case with aligning oneself with Source. To receive from Source, you must be "tuned in to Source." To attract from Source continuously and with less effort, you must maintain a continuous connection without dropped signals.

Feelings

"Feeling is conscious awareness about the vibration we're in"—*Bob Proctor*. There is a proven correlation among feelings, vibrational frequencies, and attraction. The crucial role feelings play in this necessitates the further examination of feelings. You are what you feel, so choose to be happy. Exude only positive vibes! Negative emotions will occasionally emerge, which is fine, but you must learn to control them. As much as possible, give no room to negative feelings.

I come from a part of the world where people who have a quick smile, are always happy, or seem to be delighted are viewed as if there is something wrong with them. As a result, you might hear phrases such as, "You're smiling like a fool" or "like a clown." A more serious expression has an air of importance, authority, and self-esteem and seems to imply status, power, and confidence, as if one has a great amount of respect for oneself.

The word *feeling*, in and of itself, is a noun that denotes an emotional state. It may also be referred to as a notion or attitude that is vague or even illogical. The emotions connected with this mental state are often expressed consciously or subconsciously as a reaction. So, your emotions, attitude, smile, or frown are all external indicators of how you feel on the inside.

While feelings and emotions are sometimes interchanged, as I have done here, they are two sides of the same coin. Both of them are used to assist individuals in explaining how something or someone makes them react or respond. According to Bryn Farnsworth, PhD, a postdoctoral neuroscience researcher, emotions are neurological reactions to emotional stimuli. He says, "While emotions are associated with bodily reactions that are activated through neurotransmitters and hormones released by the brain, feelings are the conscious experience of emotional reactions." They both originate from different parts of the brain, emotions from the amygdala and feelings from the neocortex, but the experience of one can create the other and vice versa. So, an emotion can create a feeling, and a feeling can create an emotion.

Exercise your God-given right to choose and make the conscious decision to feel great. Irrespective of the circumstances in your life or around you, when you feel good or optimistic about life or anything, you attract positive things to your life. Money is no different. You can't choose to despise or dislike money and then wish for it to come into your life. You may recall reading the money beliefs and thoughts about money from the survey in chapter one. Some of the responses were outright negative. Such negative thoughts and emotions will, of course, produce unpleasant or negative feelings, which work contrary to what you desire. If money is not flowing to you, it's because you're repelling it, either willingly or unwillingly. Negative thoughts create negative feelings, which in turn trigger negative actions resulting in negative outcomes. We will delve more into the power of your thoughts in the next chapter.

When you are in alignment with Source, you will feel it. It is a feeling of peace, love, kindness, meekness, gentleness, self-control, joy, hope, abundance, the absence of fear, worry, or anxiety. Whether you're feeling good or bad, you release energy that is associated with your emotions. When you are in alignment with Source, your energy is positive. When you feel good, you shine brightly, and when you're feeling negative, your brilliance dims. You can't help but have pleasant emotions when you are in tune with Source. The absence of negativity in Source makes it impossible for someone with negative emotions to connect with Source.

You're out of alignment whenever any unpleasant sentiments or feelings arise, period! You must instantly snap out of that mood by changing your thoughts, emotions, or present-moment perceptions to ones that will make you feel better. Negative thoughts or beliefs such as, "It is impossible," or "I never have enough money," do not help. While the first may create a sense of helplessness and defeat, the second can give you a sense of emptiness. You will gradually and surely become attached to the outcome of this attitude while you remain in this condition, and from there it will be a downhill slide from one negative feeling to another, culminating in a snowball effect of terrible emotions. You become more out of alignment, and you start to question why things are heading south when you're in this condition. You may be working harder, putting out effort after effort without achieving your objectives or manifesting your Desires. Positive feelings instead put you in an expectant state of the manifestation of your Desires. Consequently, a snowball of positive thoughts is set in motion—no feelings of lack or impossibilities. You start feeling as if your Desires were already realized, and you have money to do what you need. Keeping the right feelings helps you remain aligned with God, and with Him, all things are possible.

Some individuals wait for the manifestation of a Desire to feel good. Well, you may be waiting for a long time or forever and never realize your Desire. *You must feel it to receive it.* You must feel good right now in order to bring your Desire into reality. Your feelings, like a thermometer or gauge, offer you an indication of where you are on the road to realizing your Desire. It is therefore imperative that you pay close attention to where you are on the gauge.

You can't just want something without feeling it. The way the brain works is that when you think of something, your brain starts producing the chemicals necessary for the creation of the item or the thought, and the more you think about it, the more the chemicals are produced.

This means that if you want to manifest a certain outcome, then you have to be able to feel what you want, and the only way to do that is to think about the desired outcome.

When you have the feeling of the outcome, then the brain will produce the necessary chemicals, and this means that the manifestation process has already begun. Before long, the manifestation will become a reality, but only if the correct emotions are being felt while the process is taking place.

Imagine thinking about a piece of chocolate cake for ten seconds. You feel the taste in your mouth and emotions within yourself related to this thought. Then imagine going off to the store, buying and eating a cake, and having a big glass of water. Now imagine waking up in the morning and thinking about that cake again, but this time you feel no emotion on the subject. There is no reaction to the thought; it's just neutral. Does this thought still create activity? It does not, because your feelings are not responsive to it anymore.

When you detect any of the negative emotions that indicate low energy, try to activate thoughts that make you feel good and increase your energy level. What can be better than if you believe that you already have what you want? If your goal is to have more money in your bank account or to be a millionaire, begin acting as if you already have more money in your account or as if you are a millionaire now. You must be in harmony with the sentiments attributed to your Desire for it to become more likely to materialize.

We were given an assignment called "Living Your Future Life Now" during the first week of a coaching program. The first thing we had to do was to clearly express our Desires. Next, we were instructed to practice for an entire day, acting as if the objective or Desire was already realized. We had to pretend that we were experiencing our Desire now. Lastly, we were to email the coach our experience. I'd like to share my correspondence with the coach, which I've included below.

"Hi Peggy, I must say it felt a little strange, but I enjoyed every moment of my day yesterday." It felt strange because for the first time, I did not let anything stress me or be a reason for concern. I was determined and focused on feeling good that day, and I did. Make up your Mind to feel good, practice feeling good, and you will feel good.

I'm not suggesting that doing this alone will cause money to miraculously appear in your bank account or that you'll be the millionaire next door overnight. However, if you can't feel it now, you won't be able to bring your Desire into reality.

It's up to you and no one else to decide how you feel. Do not let external factors, including other people's perceptions or your own feelings, make you feel bad. You would also agree that sometimes events occur that may make you feel terrible or negative and put your ability to control unpleasant emotions to the test. Not all of these bad emotions are terrible. They may be emotions that you need to heal from or indications for your own safety. It's possible that your intuition is trying to tell you something you need to pay attention to or understand. The most essential thing is to prevent them from festering and becoming rooted in your life.

Your first response is to be aware of and acknowledge these negative feelings and not to deny them. Secondly, you must muster every effort you can to switch to a positive feeling. You might be able to change right away, but other times you may need to work on the bad feeling for a little longer and try various techniques.

Start by choosing to feel good. God is good, and when you make up your Mind to feel good, you have made up your Mind to feel God! God is at the pinnacle of expanded emotions. When we choose to feel good and vibrate with expanded emotions, we come closer to God, the Source of All. Make up your Mind to be a happy person. If you relate to the phrase *happy-go-lucky*, use it to help you stay happy and positive. I have adopted the phrase "good vibes only" as a constant reminder of my commitment to feel good all of the time, because *when I am feeling good, I feel God.* By consciously making this decision and practicing it as often as you need to, you implant it in your Subconscious Mind, after which it will eventually take over and become natural.

Start your day right, on a positive note. "This is the day which the Lord hath made; we will rejoice and be glad in it"—*Psalm 118:24.* Joining my prayer line at 6:15 a.m. is one of my daily disciplines. Unfailingly, Pastor Sola Akinlade's greeting is, "Welcome to another day, a day of life, a day of joy, a day of great peace..." Start your day right, on a positive note. Before you are out of bed, make sure to say aloud something positive to set the mood of the day. For example, "Today is going to be a great day!" Make this an unbreakable habit, and watch the miracles happen. The Law of Attraction says you create your own reality. You attract what you think about most. Your dominant thoughts will find a way to manifest themselves.

If you start your day with negative thoughts, such as "I hate my job," or "My boss is so unfair," those thoughts will set the pace for an unhappy day. You'll unknowingly attract more situations and events that reinforce those negative thoughts.

On the other hand, if you wake up and say something positive about your life, it's like water that feeds a plant. You create a positive atmosphere and attitude that will lead to more positive events throughout the day. Your Mind holds on to that thought and will produce new ideas, opportunities, and people who all contribute to making your life better.

Think of something positive. Even if it's only for a moment, *switching your thoughts* instantly stops the bad feeling from getting worse. Think of an event, a scene, or a film that you liked. Even better, imagine yourself living your future life right now. This is what Dr. Wayne Dyer refers to as *"thinking from the end."* For example, what would life feel like for you at this present moment if you were already a millionaire, if that was your Desire? What would you be doing? How would you dress? Would your swag change? Would you be traveling around the world? *Affirming words make you feel good.* For example, "I am alive unto God." Respond to situations that bring on negative feelings from a standpoint of Truth. I like to say, "I am God's best, His Masterpiece, Wonderfully and Fearfully Made in His Beautiful and Perfect Image." You can change feelings of low self-esteem by saying, "I know who I am; I am a conduit and a co-creator with Source."

Make sure the words you say are genuinely uplifting. Equally, listen and pay attention to only positive words; do not accept any negative words directed at you. Affirmations will be discussed at greater length in a later chapter.

Initiate or do something that makes you feel good. I made a resolution some years ago to go to bed feeling good after learning about what your Subconscious Mind does with your last thoughts before falling asleep. Because I enjoy real estate, particularly luxury properties, before going to sleep, I almost always watch *Behind the Gates*, a television program on high-end luxury mansions. Of course, owning one of the properties is high on my visualization board. You may do anything that makes you feel good, whether it's singing, admiring birds, cuddling your furry friend, or whatever it is. I'm not, however, implying anything illegal or unethical. At the end of the book, you'll find the seven proven bedtime routines to provide you with some direction for manifestation.

You may choose to listen to uplifting and encouraging music, and why not dance? This song I like listening to whenever I begin to doubt the outcome of a project is one you might enjoy as well: "All Things Are Ready" by Sinach. The singer is implying that everything you'll need is already there and waiting for you! This song, filled with happiness and hope, will relax you. You can almost see yourself dancing along with her. With this kind of music playing, your body automatically slows down its output of stress hormones. When you are relaxed, your chances of having a positive attitude are increased.

This relates back to the section on your origin and creation when I mentioned how God has already completed everything in creation and wants us to enjoy its manifestation and abundance. Hopefully, such encouraging words of Truth will make you feel good, knowing that you have a good chance of realizing your Desire. The Bible speaks about the excellence of joy, which is an indication that it is good to feel happy. "A merry heart doeth good like a medicine: but a broken spirit drieth the bones"—*Proverbs 17:22.*

Your *kind gestures* toward others generate good emotions. When you make someone else's day, their natural response is to return the favor. Being kind to others causes good feelings on both sides.

Count your blessings, and name them one by one. As a result, pleasant thoughts will arise in your Mind. When you are grateful and thankful, you recognize what God has done for and through you.

I am quick to laugh, and I will usually come up with a reason to chuckle in most, if not all, cases. Research has proven that laughter has emotional and physical benefits. It is said that laughter is good medicine. It not only boosts your immune system, but it also makes you feel better. *Laugh*, it feels good. Watching a great comedy show is bound to make you laugh. *Sanford and Son*, starring Redd Foxx, was a personal favorite of mine. He didn't have to say anything; just his appearance and stride got me laughing.

On an ongoing basis, it is good to *associate with people with positive mindsets.* However, when you find yourself in a position where you need to switch quickly from negative to optimistic feelings, reach out to someone, a friend or family member, who may make you laugh or offer something encouraging. I have a friend who, no matter what's going on, can make me laugh and feel wonderful practically instantly. By the time I've finished talking with her, I am uplifted.

Other switching techniques need more planning and effort. *Meditation* is one of them. It is a powerful ancient technique with a wide range of advantages, including but not limited to stress management, anxiety reduction, emotional well-being improvement, self-awareness development, and attention span extension. I must confess that I was one of those who always felt inept and a little uncomfortable when asked to participate in a meditation exercise. I found that I was losing concentration at around the five-minute mark into the meditation session. I've since discovered my own meditation approach that works well for me.

You may select from a variety of meditation techniques that are accessible online, especially on YouTube.

Train yourself to *meditate regularly.* When we think of meditation, we may picture an individual sitting in a tranquil posture with his or her arms extended as if waiting to receive something and quietly focusing on something. The Mind is focused on something or directed to achieve clarity or a greater level of awareness and understanding. For the purpose of this book, your meditation should be focused on the Source of All. If you've never meditated before or are hesitant to start, I recommend that you give it a try. You'll find that you're more motivated, confident, and self-assured. You may also feel more powerful when you realize what potential lies dormant in your Subconscious Mind. Early mornings work best for me. Sometimes, I stay in bed, and other times I go down to my study. I begin by listening to an instrumental gospel song, praising and worshipping God, before gradually drifting into a quiet state where I am solely focused on a word or idea that comes to my spirit. I do not time myself, nor do I try to figure out what to do. Instead, I allow my spirit to take the lead and halt as soon as my intellect begins changing directions or my attention wanders. If you like guided meditation, that is fine. Practice whatever type of meditation is beneficial to you. The most essential thing is that you practice meditation, which will assist you to keep a positive mindset and feel good.

Visualization is not daydreaming. Many people are daydreamers who believe they are visualizing. Just daydreaming about good things might help you shift your emotions from negative to positive, but it won't necessarily result in the manifestation of your Desire. I'm proposing that visualization be used because it's more focused on a particular result. It is very intentional, guided, and purposeful, not random, where thoughts just come to your Mind as you go about your daily activities. Simply viewing yourself with the money you want will not attract it to you. However, seeing yourself having the money you Desire and accomplishing the great things you wish to do with it for yourself, for your family, or for humanity may make you happy and produce a grin on your face. Let's take a closer look at visualization.

"Everything that's coming into your life, you are attracting into your life. And it's attracted to you by virtue of the images you're holding in your Mind. It's what you're thinking. Whatever is going on in your Mind you are attracting to you!"—*Bob Proctor*

When you visualize, you hold images in your Mind with the intention of attracting them into your life.

When you visualize, you are utilizing the power of your Mind's eye, your imagination. Everything exists in the spiritual realm before it arises in the physical world. To see what cannot be seen with the physical eye, you must use the eyes of your Mind. This may seem strange to you, but this is where you notice things not *with* your eyes but *through* them. Your creative imagination allows you to imagine and create whatever you desire. The more often your thoughts turn toward what you want, the stronger these images become. When you hold them in your Mind's eye long enough, they will begin to manifest in your physical world.

Visualization is a potent tool for eliminating negative energy and replacing it with positive energy. Visualize anything you want and make it a reality. Feel the wonderful sensation of having what you want in your life as you picture your wish.

Consider how great you'd feel if you had a better disposition. Consider how much more cheerful you'd be if your goals were realized if you had a good attitude. Whatever it is that you concentrate on with the right feelings enters your life via your emotions.

Imagine yourself being in possession of what you want before it happens in real life. This way, when it appears in physical reality, it will flow naturally.

The technique of using a vision board is very effective. A vision board is a visual depiction of your Desire(s). To keep the mental picture alive in your Mind, look at the board several times each day. Every time you look at your vision board, it produces a sense of you already having what you want, which allows it to become real!

Vision boards are most effective when you decide to use them. Once you have identified your Desire and clearly stated it, begin by putting together images of your Desire that excite you. Paste these pictures in an order that stimulates your Desire(s). You should have vivid and clear pictures or images of what you want on your vision board. Make sure all images are clearly visible. The more colorful and detailed you make your vision board, the better. The more enthusiastic your feelings, the better.

The next step is to hang it prominently in a place where you will see it every day, such as on your bedroom wall or refrigerator door! As you look at your vision board each day and night, ideally at scheduled times, concentrate on the images. Allow the positive feelings you get every time you look at your vision board to overflow into your life and allow it to magnetize what you want toward you!

Don't be shy; include people, if appropriate, on your vision board. You can also use fake dollar bills (you can buy million-dollar bills online) if you desire to manifest money. If you are computer savvy or digitally inclined, your board could be an electronic image or document.

You can simply create a reminder on your phone. I have my vision board on my phone, and it was wonderful to see that after some months of looking at it, my phone began prompting me to look at it at the same time every day.

One of the greatest examples of visualization is found in the Bible when God told Abraham, then Abram, to look up to the sky: "And the LORD said to Abram, after that Lot was separated from him, Lift up now thine eyes, and look from the place where thou art northward, and southward, and eastward, and westward: for all the land which thou seest, to thee will I give it, and to thy seed for ever." —*Genesis 13:14–15*. This is an example from another occasion: "And, behold, the word of the LORD came unto him, saying, This shall not be thine heir; but he that shall come forth out of thine own bowels shall be thine heir. And he brought him forth abroad, and said, Look now toward heaven, and tell the stars, if thou be able to number them: and he said unto him, So shall thy seed be"—*Genesis 15:4-5*. This was a visualization exercise for

Abraham and his wife, who desired to have a child. The notion of having countless children and being called the father of many nations was probably the wildest stretch of his imagination, as distant as the stars were from Earth. For someone who had never had a child and was over ninety years old, this was all but inconceivable. Despite this, he was steadfast in his belief and eventually manifested his Desire.

Abraham had to see beyond what his physical eyes could see. He didn't turn to the north, south, east, or west; he stayed on one spot and saw with the infinite range of his Mind's eye. In a subsequent verse, God said to Abraham, "Arise, walk through the land in the length of it and in the breadth of it; for I will give it unto thee"— *Genesis 13:17*. This also happened in his Mind because he could not practically walk the length and width of what he had seen in his Mind. Abraham had to feel the joy of being a father of many nations and walking the land in his Mind established the feeling of ownership, ownership of the entire land. So, when you visualize, you also must experience it in your Mind the best you can. Then you feel and live as if that which you have visualized is real.

My favorite illustration of visualization is Jacob, who, according to the book of Genesis, used his creative abilities and the principle of forming mental images, visualization, to create the desired outcome for rams under his care, resulting in them reproducing offspring according to the design before them.

Jacob was shown how to use visualization by the Angels of God in a dream, and he utilized it to bring about his desired result. "And it came to pass at the time that the cattle conceived, that I lifted up mine eyes, and saw in a dream, and, behold, the rams which leaped upon the cattle were ringstraked, speckled, and grisled. And the angel of God spake unto me in a dream, saying, Jacob: And I said, Here am I. And he said, Lift up now thine eyes, and see, all the rams which leap upon the cattle are ringstraked, speckled, and grisled: for I have seen all that Laban doeth unto thee"—*Genesis 31:10–12*.

"And Jacob took him rods of green poplar, and of the hazel and chesnut tree; and pilled white strakes in them, and made the white appear which was in the rods. And he set the rods which he had pilled before the flocks in the gutters in the watering troughs when the flocks came to drink, that they should conceive when they came to drink. And the flocks conceived before the rods, and brought forth cattle ringstraked, speckled, and spotted"—*Genesis 30:37–39*. This interesting visualization account is explained in more detail in *Genesis chapters 30–31*.

A goal card is another powerful manifestation tool. Making a goal card is an easy first step to achieving your Desire. A goal card will help you manifest your goals into reality. On one side of the card, write down what you are trying to accomplish or how you want to feel, physically and emotionally. For example, "I am a millionaire" or "I am rich." On the other side, write down the number of days you are willing to work on this goal. Maybe it's one year with weekly steps to accomplish what you want. Once you've written your goals on the card, spend some time thinking about what achieving these goals would feel like. Your goal has to be specific and in the present tense. Remember, your Subconscious Mind will work to bring these goals into reality—so the more you can imagine and feel them, the better!

Carry this card with you in your wallet, purse, or pocket. It is also helpful to make several copies of the card and put them in places where you will see them often (on your fridge, bathroom mirror, nightstand, etc.). The more frequently you are reminded of what you want, the better!

Money locating you starts with a Desire and locates you through your thoughts and feelings. You must focus on and feed your Mind with things that will strengthen and fuel your vision. To attract anything into your life, you must be vibrating at the frequency of your Desire. Your feelings will assist you in remaining on track. It's critical to focus on things that will keep your emotions high. What you give your attention to is exactly what will show up in your life.

Chapter 6 Exercise: Switching Techniques

Choose to feel good. Make a list of switching techniques you could utilize to go from negative to positive feelings. Feel free to utilize any of the solutions listed above that may work best for you, as well as additional ones if necessary.

1. _____

2. _____

3. _____

4. _____

5. _____

6. _____

7. _____

CHAPTER 7

Your Exceptionally Powerful Mind

"For as he thinketh in his heart, so is he."

—*Proverbs 23:7*

Your mindset matters. Your mindset is a set or collection of thoughts and beliefs you hold true and are established, or set, you could say. It's remarkable how you can go through life without recognizing the enormous role your mindset plays in your life. It influences your choices and actions, either for good or for bad. For this reason, if nothing else, it is critical that you begin paying closer attention to your mindset, starting with identifying your mindset. What is your mindset? For instance, you are presented with an opportunity to advance your career or business. What is the first thing that comes to your Mind? Do you see the opportunity as a threat to what you have achieved so far? Or do you perceive it as another stepping-stone to greatness and financial freedom? Your answer will give away your mindset.

In His Desire to express His wealth and limitless riches in all areas of life through you, God has equipped you with a powerful Mind. Your

Mind is the invisible gift and instrument that controls how you perceive life. The Mind and the brain are frequently interchanged; they are actually different but functionally reliant on each other. The brain is an organ in a specific area of the skull that is tangible, and the Mind, which is intangible and invisible, is a stream of activity that's conscious during our awake hours and nonconscious while we are asleep. This continuous flow of activity that is made up of thoughts, emotions, and decisions generates energy. The brain then picks up this energy and reacts in a manner that produces action. The brain merely responds to what is going on in your Mind. When you have a test done on your brain, it is these responses by the brain that are detected as neurochemical or electromagnetic changes in the brain.

A Mind that is aligned with Source can experience this abundance in any area of life. It is totally unlimited, and impossibilities are not a factor.

The Mind is one of your greatest assets. It is much more than a thinking device; it directs and controls everything you do and say, and it is the instrument you need to come into physical possession of money (and anything you desire, for that matter), so it deserves your utmost attention. Some people seem to just naturally attract money, while some never get out of the poverty cycle. What's the difference? Is it luck or chance? It's neither. It's the way you think and what you do with your Mind that makes the difference in your life. And this is never more evident than when money and prosperity are involved. You must be certain that money can come into your possession before it ever does; however, achieving this expectancy often becomes a problem because of what you have been programmed to believe. This programming may have come from your parents, relatives, friends, or society's teachings, so it is important that these ideas are carefully examined in order to establish the Truth about money for yourself. The good news is ignorance of the Truth does not mean you cannot be free; it just means that you need some information that can establish new beliefs or a new belief system within you. Later in this chapter, we will look at how to renew and manage your Mind for the expression or manifestation of these Desires in your personal life.

The irony of it all is that humanity continuously thinks it is creating new things with more knowledge, science, or artificial intelligence. In fact, all things seen, and unseen, have already been created, and man is merely discovering or becoming aware of them.

Those things that we see with our physical eyes are their physical manifestation from the spiritual. As discussed earlier, everything first exists in the spiritual, invisible realm and in our imagination before it can manifest into our physical possession. Using your Mind, you can *appropriate, lay claim to or take hold of that which you desire* and come into its *physical possession*. To manifest more money, you must first believe the preceding to be true and then begin to perceive money in this light. You must begin to visualize money in abundance, get used to seeing a great deal of it, feeling it in your life, and delighting in the sensations and sentiments of already having as much of it as you desire.

In chapter three, we discussed man's true origin and the origin of all things, Source. Source is Spirit. The three components that make up a person are the Spirit, the Soul (Mind), and the Body. Because of lack of knowledge, many people are unaware, not only of their spiritual aspect, but also of how these three components interact with one another. As the Bible says, "And ye shall know the truth, and the truth shall make you free"—*John 8:32*. When you fully grasp this Truth and understand how it is expressed in all parts of life, you may make a better connection to yourself. You'll have a new perspective on life, and an expanded view of the world will open up before your eyes. Look at this illustration for a better understanding.

Man has a twofold nature, the outer man and the inner man. The outer man is made up of the physical body and its senses of sight, touch, smell, hearing, and taste. These act like receptors or antennas. This is the part that interacts with the world and the environment. This is the

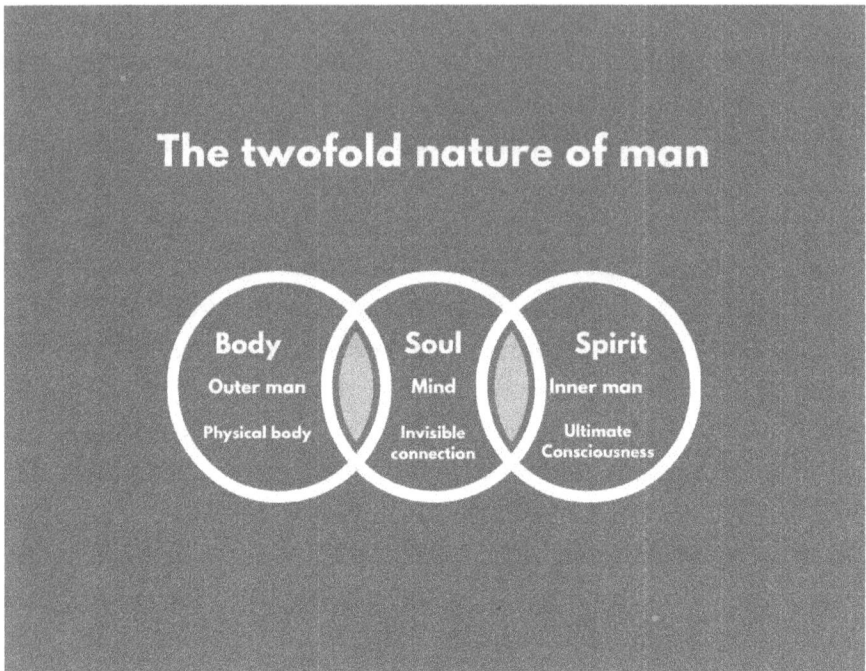

Twofold nature of man

human being. When you look in a mirror, you see your body in the physical, that is, who you may think you are: short, tall, skinny, not so skinny, figure eight, or pear-shaped. You want to describe what you see.

The other side of man is the side we do not see, and it comprises his Spirit and Soul. The spirit being is what was created in God's image because God is Spirit, and this is man's true identity. Man is a spirit being. *In other words, the real you is a spirit being living in a physical body and having a physical experience.* Soul and Mind are sometimes used interchangeably because the Soul embodies the Mind. The inner man (Spirit) and the outer man (Body) are connected by your Soul/Mind. We will use Mind to refer to Soul for simplicity. The Mind is the *invisible connection* between the Spirit and the Body (the physical). *It's crucial to note that one's life outcomes are determined by the nature (physical or spiritual) that is emphasized or focused on.* This is true since the nature determines to which world you belong and which conditions or constraints you encounter. When the Mind focuses on the physical body, reason or logic reigns supreme. The consequence of this is that when reason dominates our lives, we exist in the world and are subject to its laws and limited outcomes. Conversely, when spirituality dominates our lives, even though we exist in the world, we understand our spiritual origin, and we are subject to its laws with limitless and supernatural outcomes.

The Body, which you view on the outside, is controlled by the Mind, which you do not see. Whatever is transmitted to the Mind affects the Body's physical reality. The Mind can be likened to a fertile piece of ground or a garden, which will produce a bountiful harvest of whatever is planted in it. However, unlike a vegetable garden where we might plant tomato and pepper seeds, we plant thoughts in our Minds. You may choose what thoughts you wish to plant in your Mind, but because it is fertile, it will, without fail, produce a harvest for you.

The Mind

Now, let's take a closer look at the Mind for a moment. The Mind has been defined as "the element of a person that enables them to be aware of the world and their experiences, to think, and to feel; the faculty of consciousness and thought."—*Oxford Languages*

The Conscious Mind is the best-known component of the human Mind. It's the part that has consciousness and works with our conscious thoughts. It's also known as the Intellectual or Thinking Mind. This is the portion of your Mind where you reason and utilize your gift of choice, deciding what to let in or keep out of your Mind. I therefore like to think of it as the gatekeeper. It has the power to accept or reject any notion or idea.

Whatever you allow into your Conscious Mind enters the subconscious part of your Mind. This is where information and ideas are accepted as Truth. It is referred to as the Emotional Mind, which processes your feelings and controls 95% of your behavior and actions.

The Subconscious Mind is the Conditioned Mind, according to Bob Proctor. Whatever enters the Subconscious Mind from the Conscious Mind must be accepted. It differs from the Conscious Mind in that it does not have the ability to reason and decide whether to accept or reject thoughts that are passed to it from the Conscious Mind. Whatever is given to it (true or false) is accepted. It is not concerned with decision-making or choice; it gets straight to work making things happen based on what it has to work with—the thoughts and images that have been given to it. While it is true that the Subconscious Mind works throughout the day and night, it typically goes to work after hours when the body is asleep. This is why some have dubbed it the *Dream Maker.* The Mind works on the basic principle that it always gives you exactly what you think about.

The *Unconscious Mind* is also quite powerful, given that it may influence the course of your life without you being aware. It's made up of ideas that have been repressed or filed away, and you can't bring them up yourself. The information is also not readily available for self-reflection or introspection. For me, it's the librarian. It keeps all of your thoughts, ideas, memories, past events, and information together by sorting, organizing, and storing them. According to certain scientists, the Conscious Mind controls 5% of human behavior, with the Subconscious and Unconscious Mind controlling 95%. Others believe it is 10% and 90%, respectively.

The Conscious and Subconscious Mind will be our primary focus in this book. I liked Peggy McColl's explanation of the relationship between the Conscious and Subconscious Minds, which uses a metaphor of the Master and Servant. The Conscious Mind, based on incoming information from the five senses, communicates with the Subconscious Mind (the Servant). The Servant's duty is to follow the Master's instructions precisely, not attempting to question, validate, comprehend, or make sense of them. This is an important detail to remember, as you'll discover soon. The Conscious Mind is the boss—it directs and controls, with the Subconscious Mind acting as a faithful

Servant. In order to ensure that your Servant does exactly what you want them to do, you need to make certain they understand your instructions perfectly. Proper communication with the Subconscious Mind is an absolute necessity if we are going to get what we desire. You need to get your instructions right to make sure the Subconscious Mind understands you ... perfectly!

In chapter five, we discussed the importance of clearly stating your Desire. Here are examples of poor communication with your Servant. Would you give this set of instructions to someone who was going to perform a complex task for you? This is how many people communicate with their Subconscious Mind:

"I want to be rich." The Servant says, "OK, boss. When do you want me to start? How much money do you want?" And so, the Subconscious Mind begins working on being rich without any further instructions. You have not expressed any urgency about this Desire, so the Subconscious Mind goes about its business as usual.

"I want a new car!" The Servant says, "OK, boss. What type of car? When do you want me to start?"

"I don't want to be poor anymore." The Servant says, "OK, boss! How much time do you have?" This last instruction is interpreted by the Subconscious Mind as, "What backing can I expect from you for this endeavor? How much support will you provide?" These instructions may be interpreted by the Subconscious Mind as, "What are your priorities, Master? What must I do first?" The Subconscious Mind is now going to have to protect itself from being criticized for failure, so it might decide that it's not a good time to start—or it may start, but with difficulty. It may withhold its best efforts until you give a little more information about how serious you are about your Desire.

You've learned about the components of your Mind and how they function. So, what does this all have to do with money flowing to you? I'd say a whole lot. Let's find out.

It is up to you whether or not money locates you. It has nothing to do with who you are, where you live, or even your life experiences or the situations in your life. Keep this in mind: Money does not distinguish between individuals. It flows from one person to another, fulfilling its mission of facilitating exchange and promoting increase.

In chapter six, we examined the significance of positive emotions and how to transition from negative to positive feelings. We've also looked at the Mind, which includes your thoughts, beliefs, ideas, sentiments, and memories. Your emotions have an impact on what you bring into your life. As a result, in actuality, your Mind—more particularly, your Subconscious Mind—is the real cause behind what you attract and manifest.

Your feelings influence your vibrational frequency and affect your alignment with Source. Your feelings must be in harmony with what you desire and correspond to the natural sentiments of God. The secret to understanding this concept is the beginning of a new experience that will elevate your life to a whole new level of prosperity and success.

Many people are still waiting for God to do on their behalf what He has already done. As the singer, Sinach, said in her song, everything you'll ever want or need is right here, ready and waiting for you. She adds: "As you look in the Word and speak, you become what you see." The Word is a mirror, and when you look in it, you see your spiritual self. This is the core aspect of you that aligns with Source. Source is Spirit, after all. So, you must use your Mind to obtain what God has already given you. Paul, in his letter to the Philippians, cautions them on what to choose and what to set their minds on. He said: "Finally, brethren, whatsoever things are true, whatsoever things are honest, whatsoever things are just, whatsoever things are pure, whatsoever things are lovely, whatsoever things are of good report; if there be any virtue, and if there be any praise, think on these things"—*Philippians 4:8.*

You don't succumb to what life has dealt you in the past, as in your previous experiences or beliefs and current circumstances. Keep in Mind, this is your God-given instrument to come into possession of the abundance that is your birthright. Your thoughts and your ability to harness the power of your exceptional Mind influence what you desire and what you attract into your life. This is what I'm referring to here as *Mind Management*. This concept may be entirely new to you, but I am confident that by the conclusion of this book, you will not only be fully aware of it but you'll also have a working level of comprehension.

We will use the Stick Man model in our discussion of Mind Management. It starts with your thoughts, the thoughts in your Conscious Mind. You must be methodical in deciding what enters your Mind and what you think about in order to manage your Mind. In addition, you must be ready to block out anything that doesn't serve you. GIGO, or "Garbage In, Garbage Out," is well-known computer science jargon that we were taught while I was studying in that field. This is also true with regard to Mind Management. If you let the wrong information (trash) into your Mind, your subconscious will work on it, and the results will be trash. If you do not want trash to appear in your life, do not allow trash into your Mind.

You may not consider yourself to be a manager in the broad or professional sense of the term, but I'd like to persuade you otherwise. In fact, I'll give you the title of Operations Manager. As an Operations Manager, you collaborate with the personnel hired by your HR manager to generate high-quality goods and deliver high-quality services. You try to achieve the best possible outcomes while also maintaining your company's goals. If HR hires employees with poor work ethics and negative attitudes, the quality of goods or services will decline. To make matters worse, they'll also start influencing current workers, and your company's overall productivity will suffer. This is because HR brought in employees with the wrong mentality, who eventually produced low-quality goods and services.

If you're a visual person, I believe this explanation of the Stick Man image below will be helpful.

The bigger circle is your Mind. Remember that there are three components to your Mind, but we're only going to focus on these two: the conscious and the subconscious. Your Conscious Mind, through your

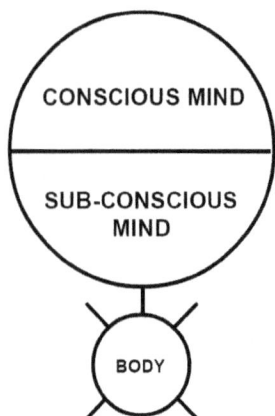

Stick Man Model -
Proctor Gallagher Institute

five senses (the projections on the Stick Man model that look like antennae), can choose what information, ideas, and beliefs to bring in—positive or negative. Your Conscious Mind, being the Intellectual and Thinking Mind, processes these in thoughts. These thoughts are transmitted to work in your Subconscious Mind. They might be thoughts that create fear, anxiety, anger, revenge, poverty, or lack, or they might promote joy, peace, hope, faith, willingness to help others, wealth, and prosperity, etc. This is where the miracle, or, if you prefer, magic, begins.

You must understand that your thoughts are the driving force behind all of your actions, decisions, and reactions. They create emotions and feelings in your Subconscious Mind, which then give rise to bodily indicators and instructions that prompt you to act or function a certain way and produce a particular result. So, whatever you think and feel will eventually result in action. The natural progression for the manifestation of your Desire will be *from your thoughts to your feelings, to your actions, and ultimately, your outcomes.*

The manifestation of your wishes might happen quickly enough for you to perhaps characterize it as mysterious or miraculous. It's common to discover that the process takes longer than you had anticipated, and you must be patient while the principle runs its course. This principle may be understood by the Law of Gestation, which states that every process has a duration that spans conception to actualization, or manifestation. A seed may, seemingly, remain dormant for days, weeks, or even months before germinating. Then it matures into a tree and begins to produce fruit after its kind over the course of many years.

When you allow particular ideas to enter your Mind, they are imprinted or impressed on your Subconscious Mind over time. It's often the case that you're completely unaware of what goes on behind the scenes. Those ideas and, more significantly, other people's thoughts (whether correct or incorrect) become your convictions. I'd also like to remind you that everything contains energy, so the knowledge you accept in is energy flowing into you, being imprinted on your Subconscious Mind, and eventually manifesting as results. Negative thinking and ideas produce bad or negative energy. Low energy depletes your emotions, resulting in low vibrational frequencies. By now, I'm sure you've figured out what happens next; you'll receive negative effects or results, and vice versa. Garbage in, garbage out! You can't plant carrots and harvest corn. In fact, every time you plant a kernel of corn, it produces additional ears of corn. "Be not deceived; God is not mocked: for whatsoever a man soweth, that shall he also reap"—*Galatians 6:7*.

Let's look at the metaphor of cultivation to help you grasp the fundamental idea of Mind Management. A farmer will generally follow these steps to get the greatest yield: till the soil, fertilize it, and then sow the seed. The farmer waters the seed after it has been sown (and rain falls on it) in order to improve the soil's condition and create a more favorable growth environment. After a while, the farmer will have to attend to the developing crop, as weeds may grow that he must remove. If the requirements listed above are not satisfied, the harvest may fall short of the farmer's hopes. Consider your Mind to be the soil. You must care for it in the same way a farmer cares for his or her soil. Thoughts are like seeds planted in your Mind by the farmer. The thoughts you expose it to will nourish or starve it. Negative ideas about money and limiting beliefs can strangle the seed or growing crop, resulting in scarcity and poverty.

Consequently, to attract money, you must learn to manage your Mind in such a way that it can produce what you desire and what you'd love—and not the opposite. How do you go about this, you may ask?

When things don't go the way they'd planned, some people frequently point fingers at a variety of causes. The farmer also has natural elements to blame for a poor yield. We're aware that a number of variables may cause what we want to happen to be delayed or not materialize at all. My objective is to assist you to redirect your attention away from such things or circumstances. "While we look not at the things which are seen, but at the things which are not seen: for the things which are seen are temporal; but the things which are not seen are eternal"—*2 Corinthians 4:18.*

There is no comparison or rivalry here, but I'd like to point out that many people are subjected to the same or similar circumstances or factors. In Philippians 2:13, we are reminded that: "For it is God which worketh in you both to will and to do of His good pleasure." If you are connected to Him, you may be subjected to similar circumstances; but still be able to manifest your desire. *Source is not subject to circumstances.* No circumstances or factors could obstruct the Creator's beauty, abundance, power, and increase in the Universe. Don't allow a negative attitude to stifle the flow of prosperity into your life. Before you fall into that trap, pay close attention to the following section.

If you've wanted to attract more money into your life but money isn't finding its way to you, something has to change. You must *renew your Mind.* You might have to till the soil again, change nutrient doses, plant higher-quality seeds, water the soil more often, or remove weeds in order for your plants to thrive and bear fruit.

In his book, *The Power of Your Mind*, Rev. Chris Oyakhilome likens the human Mind to a computer hard drive, using the example of a computer hard drive to illustrate this aspect of the powerful Principle of Mind Management. A computer's hard drive is where all of its data is stored. To improve data retrieval speed, a hard drive must be defragmented or maintained from time to time. You may have to delete temporary files and remove old programs that are taking up too much hard drive space in order to improve overall performance. Your Mind is the same. There is a degree of denial that goes into this process. However, to be effective, you must erase and "uninstall" any negative ideas or beliefs. It's like starting over from scratch on a clean slate. It reminds me of when I was in primary school. We used what were known as arm boards or black slate boards at the time. We wrote our homework on the slates using white chalk. Sometimes, by the time we got home, most of the information had been rubbed off accidentally or on purpose. We had to get the information from other children because there was no previous reference on a clean slate, no prior record of what was there before. That meant starting anew. Sometimes, to eradicate all of those negative and limiting ideas that have taken residence in your Mind, it is necessary to erase everything and start over.

We acquire much information daily that is the foundation of our thoughts, beliefs, and mindset. It's an enormous task to completely erase, reverse, or uninstall several years' worth of information, thoughts, and beliefs. It is, however, very doable, and will result in a totally transformed you. Your Mind can also be compared with a car engine, and it must be maintained, tuned, and possibly cleaned on a regular basis in order for it to function properly and at its peak capacity. It's worth noting that, in his letter to the Romans, Apostle Paul advised them as follows: "And be not conformed to this world: but *be ye transformed by the renewing of your mind*, that ye may prove what is that good, and acceptable, and perfect, will of God"—*Romans 12:2*.

Renewing your Mind is a conscious and deliberate endeavor. It takes commitment and discipline. For some, it will be a quick process; for others, it will be a slow one. While you are attempting to improve your beliefs or emotions, you will undoubtedly face several challenges that will cause you to doubt what you're doing and attempt to persuade you to stay with the same mindset or keep the same opinions that are holding you back or preventing you from achieving what you want. Your Mind has already built a wall or an impediment if you can't conceive and believe that money may be produced in abundance (whatever the amount). Money, of course, will continue to circulate and locate the individual who believes differently.

Begin by taking command of and accepting responsibility for your thoughts. *Your results are the creation of your own thinking.*

How you think about things, your beliefs, how you approach problems, and the kind of life you live are all products of your mindset. There is a direct correlation between your mindset and the amount of money that enters your life.

Take a look at your life right now. What would you say if you had to describe your mindset? What phrases would you use? This chapter exercise will be helpful and may be a good place to start if you're not sure. Of course, I have a wealth of additional information to offer on the subject that would be too extensive for this book. See the Premiere Destiny page at the end of the book or go to www.premieredestiny.com more information.

A variety of mindsets exists, and each is determined by different variables. For the purposes of this book, we will limit ourselves to the fact that these various mindsets may be divided into two categories: positive and negative. Congratulations if you have a positive mindset! Keep at it, and sooner or later, as you apply the ideas in this book, what you desire will eventually come to pass. Having the right mindset is more than half the battle won!

I commend you for completing this exercise, even if you discovered that you have a fixed, restricting, or negative mindset. As the saying goes, "You cannot manage what you don't measure." You've taken the first and most critical step. You have become aware. Thanks to this awareness and knowledge, you may now take appropriate measures to cultivate a more positive mindset.

You want to *start thinking differently*. It's time for you to make a deliberate decision, backed by resolve and discipline, to cut off or limit your exposure to things that might generate negative and limiting ideas. You must also start encouraging good and growth ideas at the same time. The Word of God is extremely clear when it comes to the type of things to think about: "Finally, brethren, whatsoever things are true, whatsoever things are honest, whatsoever things are just, whatsoever things are pure, whatsoever things are lovely, whatsoever things are of good report; if there be any virtue, and if there be any praise, think on these things"— *Philippians 4:8*. If we are to attract anything from Source, we must do things in a particular way, God's way. If our farmer in the example above wishes to harvest peas the following year, he will not plant corn; he must alter what he sows in order to achieve his goal.

You exchange your thoughts, *replacing negative thoughts with positive thoughts*. People who believe money is bad will have a tough time adopting positive money ideas. This belief will put your Desire and capacity to attract money into your life to the test. I've included some pointers at the end of the book to assist you in getting started.

Visualization may aid in the renewal of your Mind by replacing negative ideas with positive ones. Visualization is a very productive way to replace your negative thoughts with some positive ones. It's easy after some practice! It is a good new habit that has many benefits and can replace negative thoughts if done regularly. Focus your thoughts to perceive things from a different perspective and see all the possibilities that exist. Visualize your Desire already realized. You should replace all those negative thoughts about yourself with something more positive, and it'll motivate you instead! As you keep believing in yourself, unpleasant ideas will be supplanted with positive ones. Reminisce on who you are and know your true identity and potential. Maintain this awareness at all times, even when situations become difficult. As you keep these beliefs reinforced, thoughts such as "I am destined to prosper," "I too can be rich," "It is my birthright to be rich," "I have an endless supply," "I am not trying to make it ," and "I was born made," will begin to take hold, while negative thoughts, such as "I can never make it, so why try?" or "I just don't have what it takes to succeed in life," will begin to vanish.

To better understand how replacing negative thoughts with positive thoughts may aid in renewing your Mind, see the accompanying illustration.

Continue focusing on Truths and reinforcing those positive beliefs by allowing in more positive thoughts. *Affirm* what you believe, not what you feel. The more you focus on something, the more your Mind believes it. These positive beliefs become your mindset. Your mindset is what's set in your Mind that predetermines your responses to situations and, consequently, your actions, experiences, and results. You control your Mind, not the other way around. Your Mind is your servant. Give it the right tools and set it to work, and it will produce the right results. Your mindset, on the other hand, is what controls you.

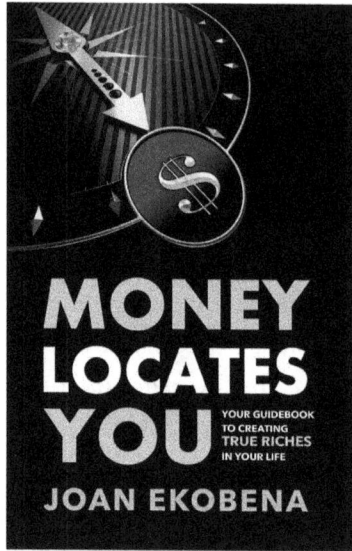

Augmented Reality video on the Mind
Please refer to the first page for instructions

Celebrate each accomplishment. You may be surprised that things begin to shift when you start thinking differently. You may be thrilled to discover that people around you have noticed and, in some cases, adjusted their interactions with you as a result of your new perspective. If the reaction is positive, fantastic! If not, you're on the correct path; just keep going and celebrate as you go.

Positive expectations are a must. Don't wake up expecting something terrible to happen. Start your day on the bright side with a positive attitude, anticipating the best. With the intended result in Mind, you must have an expectation that things will work out for the best.

Your thoughts are powerful and a powerful tool for manifestation, because like a magnet, they draw to you whatever they resemble. If you think about having an abundant supply of money, then your Mind will attract abundance; if you think about poverty and hardship, then that is what you'll get! There is no doubt whatsoever that we become what we think. Thoughts affect us at every level: physically, psychologically, and emotionally. They affect our bodies and minds in different ways and can be passed on from generation to generation as well as throughout eternity via Soul-Consciousness.

Thought is a powerful tool for manifestation because all human experience begins with thought, and it is also powerful because we have been conditioned from an early age to let our minds run wild, unchecked by reason or logic.

The Mind is a powerful tool for manifestation. The Mind works like a camera; whatever you focus on gets processed by the brain. The things that you focus on and think about most consistently will become the dominant force in your life.

Negative thoughts bring about negative outcomes, while positive thoughts bring about good ones. Whatever you think with your Mind will produce the corresponding result. To see change in any area of your life, you must first undergo internal change through positive thinking and strong affirmations. That is how you attract money in your life and create your world—one thought at a time!

It is important to understand and know this: Your Subconscious Mind cannot tell what's real and what's imagined. You may program your powerful Mind to help you achieve a goal if you think about yourself achieving it often enough until it feels true.

If you've been practicing affirmations and visualizations but nothing has manifested in your life, there's a good chance something is getting in the way on an internal level. Because of one reason or another, your strong Mind has linked negative energy with your goal or Desire in such a manner that when it hears the affirmation or sees imagery related to the planned transformation, rather than allowing it to do so through repetition of action, it redirects you toward unde-sirable outcomes! You might start sabotaging yourself without even realizing it.

You must learn how to renew your Mind by erasing those old associa-tions and replacing them with positive and powerful new ones.

Keep your Mind occupied by focusing on truthful thoughts and exposing your senses to those things that will generate good ideas. Make an effort to *resist negative thoughts* that may arise by clinging to Truths and resisting the urge to indulge yourself in false notions. We will discuss some of these notions further in the next chapter. Some television pro-grams or news networks may be breeding grounds for negative informa-tion that may drain your energy and feed you negative ideas. Pay attention to the programs, news channels, music, events, and even friends that may promote negativity, and avoid or minimize your exposure to them. Don't allow negative ideas to take hold. They'll come and go, but don't let them grow roots. "You cannot stop birds from flying over your head, but you can stop them from building a nest in your hair."—*Martin Luther*

The following exercise challenges you to think about various types of mindsets, which are referred to as fixed or growth mindsets. You're likely to find that you have more mindsets than you imagined. I believe this is one of the most fascinating exercises in the book, and you may be shocked to learn about a new side of yourself.

Social	Fear	Growth	Business	Lazy
Quick to start a conversation with strangers and enjoys hanging out with others	Usually worries about what can go wrong. Over analytical	Enjoys learning new things, desires to improve themselves & embraces challenges. Do not see limitations. Failure doesn't discourage them.	Have a drive to serve and help others & enjoy taking calculated risks	Lacks desire and struggles with discipline. They do the bare minimum and see everything as too difficult. No confidence in themselves.
Dreamer	**Envy**	**Gratitude**	**Creative**	
Full of imagination, creativity, and vision. Spends more time daydreaming than actually executing your plans	Tend to be covetous, feel inferior, have low self-esteem, have feelings of resentment. Looks for happiness from external sources.	Appreciate things more and look beyond themselves and seeing how good things really are. Optimistic outlook on life.	See things differently. Embrace new ideas and not afraid of failure. Believe intelligence not fixed with to intelligence than exam grades. Curious and tenacious in pursuit of a solution.	

Short term	Abundance	Fixed	Scarcity	Confident
Engages in short term solutions to long term problems. May have some degree of low self-esteem or anxiety, overcautious and easily give up. There is a fear of failure.	The world is abundant with possibilities, therefore there's no need to compete. Positive outlook for better and greater things and outcomes. Abundance is not limited to wealth and material possessions.	Things are good or bad. No need to change if everything seems fine. Content to stick with what they know. Don't believe in their own talent and potential, therefore struggle to learn more.	For one person to win, another must lose. Limited resources or opportunities to go around. Rely on competition rather than collaboration. Life is difficult, and there is never enough for everyone, so everyone for themselves.	Possess emotional and psychological strength to deal with any problems which arise. Believe in themselves with an air of self-assuredness to stand up to intimidating challenges.

Productive	Greed	Leader		
Positive thinking, experiences are opportunities to learn. Look at events as an educational opportunities. Ignores distractions and focuses on what needs doing and gets it done. Open-minded and holds themselves accountable.	Experiences the need to possess more to feel fulfilled. Never gets enough of anything even when it is wasteful but can't help themselves. Typically, over-estimate the value of their possessions.	Confident. Willing to speak up for their beliefs. Open minded but do not follow without question. Not people pleasers. Decisions are based on their understanding of what is best for people, not people want.		

Chapter 7 Exercise: Identify Your Mindset

CHAPTER 8

The Power of Words

———— ❦ ————

"So shall my word be that goeth forth out of my mouth: it
shall not return unto me void, but it shall accomplish that
which I please, and it shall prosper in the thing
whereto I sent it."

—Isaiah 55:11

On July 21, 2018, a pleasant and lively discussion about children and how they sometimes make life-changing decisions without consulting their parents swiftly became an argument over the power of words. One of the friends had just made a negative remark about his son. Somehow, this very educated individual made a few comments, the last of which was, "This kid is insane." I immediately requested that he stop using such hurtful and damaging words in reference to his child. He burst out laughing, brushing me off, and actually ridiculing my response. "That was a joke," he stated, and we all knew it was a joke. Of course, we brushed off the comment and continued to talk about anything else. The lack of awareness of the power of our words is what I'm driving at. Whether or not you are aware of it, your words have the power to chart your destiny and determine what you manifest in life. Words, like everything else, have energy and return to where they came from. Your words affect the entire Universe, not just the individual you are talking to or about. If you knowingly or unknowingly put the wrong kind of energy into the world through your words, the results can be negative, and it may take some time before you realize the mistake.

Words have been studied and documented in depth on the influence they have on a child's developing brain. Negative or damaging phrases such as "You're stupid" or "useless kid" may harm a child's self-esteem and how they perceive themselves for the rest of their lives. On the other hand, words that are good and constructive, such as "You are smart," "You are the best," and "I am proud of you," have precisely the opposite impact. I was fortunate to grow up in a family that showed me love and optimism. We were challenged financially, but words of love and encouragement saw us through the toughest times.

My grandmother, a woman of great faith in God, never failed to remind me and my siblings about the importance of being aware that we were very blessed and had limitless potential. I'm certain that this was the foundation of my mindset.

Positive and negative words have an influence on people of all ages. Adults' morale, self-image, confidence, and other traits are positively affected by positive words directed toward them, while negative and critical words may demean and elicit the most negative reactions in some.

I am thankful for the opportunity to share with you the Truth about this idea, which I refer to as *the miracle of your words*. You may inadvertently undermine the strength of your words in much the same way as my friend. You might be someone who thinks that if you make a remark in jest, it isn't a big deal. I hope that by the end of this chapter, your viewpoint or conviction will be totally changed for the better.

"Death and life are in the power of the tongue: and they that love it shall eat the fruit thereof"—*Proverbs 18:21*. According to this verse, we'll eat the fruit of our words. Words are like seeds, and as soon as they leave your mouth, they have been sown and will yield a crop. Do you recall our earlier farming-and-seeds metaphor? Your words can make or break and have the power of life and death. If you sow words of prosperity, you will be prosperous. If you sow words of health, you will enjoy good health. That is because what you say has the ability to birth anything you say. Those words are now alive, and they'll give you what you said. The comparison is made between the tongue and the rudder of a ship. A rudder is insignificant in comparison to the size of a ship, and your tongue is small in relation to the rest of your body. A rudder is a small piece, usually at the back of a ship or plane, used to steer a ship or plane in a certain direction. The tongue is comparable to the rudder in that it guides your life in much the same way as a rudder does for a ship.

Are you willing to eat the results of your words? Are you allowing yourself to be your own enemy? You've done everything correctly. You're aligned with Source, vibrating at the same frequency, and you want to attract one million dollars so that you may purchase a yacht. You've gotten your Mind and emotions in order, and you're already visualizing having a wonderful time on your yacht, sailing the waters and enjoying nature. You already have some fantastic ideas, and you're getting started. Somewhere along the line, you encounter difficulties. If you say, "I don't see this happening," "What was I thinking?" or "I will never be able to pull this off," you have just become your worst enemy with your own words. If you let these thoughts fester, you'll soon come to accept them as reality. You've introduced death into your Desire, project, or goal by doing so. With your own words, you have activated *success blockers*. It won't be long before things start going wrong, and the Desire may well die a natural death. Because you stopped it in its tracks with your choice of words, the money may never locate you.

Don't oppose yourself and become your own enemy by speaking contrary to God's Word. *Choose your words wisely*, and practice speaking positive words, words of life.

You have no control over what people say to you, and you can't always predict what will be said. But you do have the power to and should immediately reject any negative comments addressed toward you. Remember, once your Conscious Mind gives these comments the green light into your Subconscious Mind, your Subconscious Mind runs with them to the finish line, realizing them. Negative remarks may be spoken in ignorance, fear, or jealousy, for example. You will retain control and negate any adverse effects they might have by rejecting them or utilizing them to inspire you. You reject negative words or statements by not agreeing with them and instead refuting them with positive ones, ensuring that the positive words remain in your Mind.

There's a tale of a deaf frog who wanted to reach the top of a tall tree. He had considered this difficult undertaking for a long time. He gradually overcame his fears, and one day he had the courage to face his burning Desire and resolved to climb this enormous tree. His friends were terrified that he would fall to his death as he ascended the tree. So, they began shouting at him, trying to persuade him not to attempt such a deadly feat. He was unable to hear what they were saying because he was deaf, so he didn't realize what they were saying. He instead interpreted their shouts as encouragement, believing that his friends were encouraging him to reach the top. You must be deaf to any discouraging words that will cause you to give up trying to realize your Desire.

It might be challenging for you to act deaf to negative or limiting words directed at you, but it is considerably easier than what we're going to discuss next: the words that we speak to ourselves or about ourselves. What I'm talking about here is not an internal monologue (thoughts which you read about in the previous chapter), but rather spoken language, what we verbalize. Many people have thwarted the manifestation of their aspirations by speaking negative and limiting words about themselves and their circumstances.

In many cases, they are unaware of the principle that the power of life and death resides in words. Positive words create life, while negative words destroy it. "For by thy words thou shalt be justified, and by thy words thou shalt be condemned"—*Matthew 12:37*. You utilize the creative energy of words when you speak positively. Words have life force. The power in words has the capacity to construct or destroy, encourage or intimidate. The energy is also audible and vibrational. What is created in the physical is determined by the vibration. In the previous chapter, you learned about your incredibly strong Mind and how much power your thoughts have. Your words, on the other hand, create open and bold affirmations that are acknowledgments of your innermost thoughts to Source.

God spoke words in the creation narrative: Let there be light, and there was light. God of Supreme and Infinite Intelligence and Power might have simply conceived the world into being without speaking a single word, but He did speak. In my opinion, this has two advantages: First, it reminds us of the creative power of words, and second, it serves as a reminder that we should use our words to create positive change in the world. You may think, "Well, I'm not God." However, keep in mind that you were formed after His image, and you have the creative capacity just like Him, and it's with your words.

With your own words, you pave the way to your next and higher level, because your words determine your future. "Thou shalt also decree a thing, and it shall be established unto thee: and the light shall shine upon thy ways"—*Job 22:28*.

Who and what you are today is largely the result of words you and others have uttered throughout your life at some point. You see, words do not result in nothingness. They are like seeds; they bear fruit. The fruit is always found after the kind of word. According to Sinach, "When you look in the Word and you speak, you become what you see." You will become what you see if you look in the mirror of God's Word and speak what you see, which is precisely what He stated about you. His words are backed by Divine power and ability. Your ideas will eventually line up or be aligned with His thinking when you speak in accordance with His Word. Put this gift to good use by speaking in line with the Word, because anything else will produce unwanted results.

Your words define your reality. With the two short but extremely powerful words *I am*, you describe yourself to others, establishing who you are. If you tell someone, "I'm an idiot," you are both telling others and confirming to yourself that you are stupid. Think about the words that follow your "I am" statement carefully. Consider them to be prophetic since you're uttering them into reality.

You must also *speak with conviction*. God reminds us in *Hebrews 13:6* to speak boldly and confidently because of what He has said: "So that we may boldly say, The Lord is my helper, and I will not fear what man shall do unto me." You should say boldly and in faith because it is Truth. When you speak Truth, your words are not empty; they will achieve their purpose. If I may ask the question: If you believe Source is the origin of all, seeking to express His abundance through you, why don't you boldly affirm and declare what He has said about you? It will be self-defeating and detrimental to your success if you speak words that contradict what He has said about you. Don't give it a second thought if your friends or family don't understand what you're saying or affirming. God's wisdom is foolishness to man. Even if you don't have the cash in your account, see yourself rich and say you're wealthy. God said, "Let the poor say I am rich." If you desire to manifest money, you must speak words consistent with financial increase or wealth, irrespective of what your current circumstances are. There is abundance of everything, and this might come to you as a surprise. So, if you're battling or coping with any form of lack or poverty, you're settling for less. Why settle for less when there is abundance? Why not *flip the script* and use *affirmations*, the Law of Positive Statements, to attract money into your life? This is your chance to turn things around, flip the script, and start speaking the right words if you have been ignorantly or deliberately making detrimental statements about your financial position. You may do so by stating Truths about your financial situation. When words have been spoken, they cannot be retracted; the impact of those words can be reduced or reversed only by speaking words with the opposite effect.

Affirmations condition your spirit and must therefore be positive and true. As you continue to repeat affirmations on a daily or more frequent basis, the words you choose will begin to alter, and you'll eventually reverse the script of negative words to positive language. Affirmations are a way of boldly stating or believing what God has asked you to boldly state.

Money Affirmations

Don't be trapped by what you've long accepted as Truth or what your present circumstances suggest. Let your Mind accept this principle.

You have been given everything concerning life and godliness. This is what God has decreed. Your duty is to respond by acknowledging and agreeing to what has been stated. I particularly like this affirmation by Bob Proctor: "I am so happy and grateful now that … money comes to me in increasing quantities through multiple Sources on a continuous basis."

If you believe you were born rich, say so. Don't let your present financial status lead you to believe and declare anything different.

Whatever negative ideas you may have about money, this is your opportunity to begin reversing them. Whatever words you may have said in the past that might have stifled the flow of money into your life, reverse them, and begin affirming the right words now. As you repeat these positive affirmations to yourself, you are impressing them on your Subconscious Mind, and they'll be accepted as reality. Keep in mind that the Subconscious Mind can accept only what is presented to it, and it is unable to reject anything. Here are some affirmations you may immediately try. Of course, this is not a comprehensive list, but it will get you started. The Affirmation Train, in the final chapter, includes even more affirmations for you.

- I am destined to prosper.
- My income exceeds my spending.
- It is natural and easy for me to prosper.
- Financial prosperity is God's will for me.
- I am not poor; I am rich.
- It's okay for me to desire more money.
- I deserve more money, and it flows to me freely.
- Money comes to me from different Sources.
- I have an endless supply of money.

Bring your thoughts into obedience of the Word, and speak your Desires into reality.

Think about your experiences with money in the past.

Make a list of any negative beliefs you may have regarding money.

With your updated understanding of the power of words, write your new belief or affirmation against each negative belief.

Chapter 8 Exercise: Old versus New beliefs

Old negative belief	New positive belief

Are You Ready to Receive?

———— ❧ ————

"Ask for what you want and be prepared to get it."

—*Maya Angelou*

I grew up in a house without a plumbing system for running water, and we had to go out every day to get drinking water from a river that wasn't particularly clean. The town I grew up in was very hot but occasionally had torrential rains. The children in my neighborhood took advantage of such opportunities to collect water, cleaner water that was used for several days. We were glad because it cut down on the number of trips we had to make to the river. As the clouds got darker, in anticipation of the rain, we'd get our containers ready and even put them out before the rains came. Water was collected by placing large containers in strategic locations to catch the cleanest and greatest amount of water. Whenever rain fell, we put our containers out and collected water, then stored it.

From this experience, we can learn a few things about receiving that we'll cover in this chapter.

- Giving: You must give to receive. This is law, the Law of Receiving. You must give the Universe your containers to hold the water from the rain.

- The amount of water you collect is determined by the size of your containers.

- You must take action by putting out your containers. Sometimes you may get wet in doing so. You'll miss out on free, clean water if you don't put your containers in the right place at all times. You can get two or more gallons of drinking water for *free* every day without having to lift a finger!

- Prepare to receive. Have your container ready.

- Be expectant. Expectation is a powerful force in the Universe. Expect to receive your wish.

- We had to repeat this process of getting our containers ready, and strategically positioning them whenever the rains came, to collect water.

Money, like the rain, is abundant in the Universe. Give the Universe your bucket, and it will be filled with your Desires.

So, have you completed everything suggested in this book so far? If so, are you prepared to receive what is coming your way? Everything in the Universe has energy, and there is a continuous circulation and flow of energy that must be uninterrupted if problems are to be avoided.

There is a law called the Law of Receiving. According to this law, giving precedes receiving. One can also see the Law of Cause and Effect and the Law of Polarity at work here. According to the Law of Polarity, everything has an opposite. There cannot be any giving without receiving. This law operates through exchange and demands the following: Giving and Gratitude.

- Giving (When you give, you open yourself to the abundance of the Universe.)

- Gratitude (This law calls for you to be grateful, even when you have not manifested your Desire.)

Receiving is giving. This may seem counterintuitive because in giving, you are letting go of something. This is true in the physical, but not so in the spiritual. The Principle of Giving and Receiving is a spiritual Truth that goes against the grain of how people think things happen in life.

We learn to receive by giving. Giving attracts receiving and gives you the freedom and means to improve your life and receive the abundance of money.

When we give, we make someone happy, or we make ourselves happier. When we give with joy, we feel even better than before! One thing about being happy is that it's contagious. It can be very hard not to be affected by other people's happiness because the frequency of their energy affects yours so easily!

There are different attitudes about giving. Some people think they must give until it hurts—until they have no more food or goods left or until they don't have enough money or time for themselves. They believe this kind of generosity will somehow earn them great rewards in the future. But they can give without this exhausting kind of giving, which is truly self-defeating.

You don't have to give of yourself until you are empty before the Universe will fill you up again. You can also learn to give in a way that will ensure that your storehouse will always be full, overflowing with the riches of the Universe! By receiving God's gifts and blessings, we will begin to live abundantly now!

Let us proceed on our journey together. Receiving may seem difficult at first because it requires some work on your part, but after some practice, you'll find it's easy and even fun to receive what is rightfully yours! When you are attuned to universal law, complying with the rules of life, you'll see how easy it is to succeed in receiving whatever you desire.

As you give, you receive a smile of appreciation, a thank you, a hug, etc. from the receiver. The one receiving, on the other hand, is allowing the giver to receive. "The one who waters shall himself be watered." I come from a culture where people always want to give when they receive something. It doesn't matter if it is of equal value or worth. Growing up, when someone visited us and brought, say, food in a basket or whatever the container was, that basket did not go back to the giver without something in it. I remember my grandmother musing over what she would put in the basket before returning it to the giver. I suppose she didn't want to be the one to interrupt the constant circulation in the Universe.

The secret to receiving is in the giving, the giving of material or non-material things, self, or service. Giving is a prerequisite for receiving. "There is *one* who scatters, yet increases more; And there is *one* who withholds more than is right, but it *leads* to poverty"—*Proverbs 11:24 (New King James Version)*.

A recent study published in *Social Cognitive and Affective Neuroscience* identified that when we observe kindness in others, there is increased activity in regions of our brain associated with reward. We recognize that we have just done a good deed, and thus increase the activity in regions of our brain associated with reward.

Likewise, when we receive kindness from others, there is an increase in activity in these same regions of the brain. In this case, the receiver recognizes they are being cared for by another individual, which generates a feeling of pleasure within their own brains. Both giver and receiver produce similar patterns of brain activity from simply witnessing or receiving kind acts from one another.

What are you giving, and what are you receiving? For some people, the word *giving* conjures up thoughts of money or material things. Your gift might be tangible or intangible. It might be a compliment, assistance, or something to eat. "Give, and it shall be given unto you; good measure, pressed down, and shaken together, and running over, shall men give into your bosom. For with the same measure that ye mete withal it shall be measured to you again"—*Luke 6:38*. Whenever possible, *give generously*. When done correctly, the Law of Receiving will not fail you. Giving is like a seed that is planted and produces a larger harvest. The conditions must be right for it to grow and bear fruit

Give with the right intention. The intention of giving must be pure. Giving must be done for the right reasons. If you give because someone else gave to you and expects something in return, you are caught in an endless cycle of lack and scarcity, like a treadmill that continues to move but makes no progress.

Giving must be accompanied by the understanding that when we give freely or selflessly, gifts will undoubtedly return to us since God delights in a giver who is also generous. The more we give without seeking anything in return—even praise, appreciation, and other forms of flattery—the greater our reward will be. King Solomon became extremely wealthy by giving extravagantly out of a love for wisdom and knowledge. Some give to impress or expect a favor in return. *Give freely with no strings attached.* Do not mistake this for a business transaction, for instance, giving a loan to a friend or anyone, for that matter. In such a case, you would expect to get paid back, sometimes with interest.

Don't be insincere or self-serving. Let your passion for assisting others, making a difference in someone's life, or enhancing the world show through. Give out of a genuine desire to assist or make a difference to someone or to the world. Giving should not be done with a sullen demeanor, reluctantly, or out of guilt. It's more about how you give than how much you give.

You have become a slave of money if you find yourself resisting giving or being dissatisfied with having to give anything, whether material or physical. "God delights in a giver who is happy," but not someone who is constantly concerned about what he may receive. Giving should be unconditionally generous, yet it must not be passive, because gift-giving has the potential to expand into areas beyond your wildest dreams. Once you start giving unconditionally, be prepared to receive more than you ever dreamed of because giving is receiving! We all have the giving gene, and we need to switch on giving in our lives. Your powerful giving fingerprint can motivate you into giving more, giving better, and giving with joy. Feel the joy in giving, give freely, and receive graciously. Receiving is a natural consequence of giving.

In the section on visualization, I suggested you have a clear mental image of what you want. In doing so, you're giving your Subconscious

Mind something to work with. If you give your Subconscious Mind something positive to work with, it will return goodness. But be careful! If you give your Subconscious Mind negative thoughts, then it will also return negative outcomes. Here again, we see that if you give your Subconscious Mind something to work with, it will return the favor. We see the Law of Cause and Effect at work here—the cause being the mental image you give your Subconscious Mind and the effect being the manifested outcome.

Give consistently. Make it a habit to give regularly. You receive constantly if you give consistently. Remember, energy is always flowing in and out of everything we do. Source expects us to give at a specific time, season after season or year after year.

Some Christians practice consistent giving through tithing, whereby they give at certain intervals throughout the year. Some think tithing is giving away money. It is not about giving money away; it is about sowing a seed, investing in your future. The Source of All, God, places no limits on His ability to respond to the seed sown by those who do not doubt Him. If we sow our seed in such a way as to expect an abundant harvest, we will surely reap just that. While this may not be readily understood by some, even those who give, they are accomplishing two things. Firstly, they are aligning themselves with God, and secondly, declaring their faith in God; faith in the God who says He'll supply according to His riches in heaven. Giving is a form of energy exchange. When you give, you are giving out your energy and drawing in what you need. When the flow is complete, the law is done for that period. If we want to continue receiving from Source, we must continue to give.

Before leaving the idea of giving, I'd like to caution you about the following. Before giving, keep in mind that the rewards will return to you in good measure, so be mindful of what you give and also to whom or to what cause you give. You should give in accordance with God's Word and nature of increase to promote a greater good, to increase or develop a worthy ideal, and to better society. If not, your giving will be contrary to God's nature, comparable to throwing your pearls to the pigs, which will not result in an increase.

Practice gratitude. Consider how many blessings you have received in comparison with the rest of the world. If you took the total number of days you've been alive so far (365 multiplied by your age), you'd be grateful and appreciate that you got up on each one of those days. So be grateful for the gift of life itself; 163,898 people die every day. Whether or not you have glasses, you may be thankful that you are able to read this book. Appreciate your eyesight.

Gratitude is defined as a disposition to recognize and return kindness. One of the most common ways to express gratitude is simply to say thank you. It recognizes the other person's good and makes them feel valued. Gratitude helps you maintain a positive outlook toward others and life in general.

Gratitude is an acknowledgment of having or being, and it's an emotional state in which you feel appreciation for what you have or are. It shows that you have it or are experiencing it, now, in your current reality. You'll receive more of what you acknowledge to have, to feel, or to be.

It creates a feeling and consciousness of *having* and subdues the feeling of *lack*. Gratitude spreads happiness to both the giver and receiver. According to Wallace D. Wattles, the Law of Gratitude is the natural principle that action and reaction are always equal and in opposite directions.

Gratitude can also be demonstrated through thanksgiving and praise. In chapter seven, I covered how you should think of your words as seeds. Your affirmations, praise, and thanksgiving must be used to water these seeds. Thanksgiving is observed annually in the United States, Canada, Grenada, St. Lucia, and Liberia. It is derived from the colonial harvest dinner of 1621 in the United States. During this time, American families rejoice and give thanks for the harvest and previous year's blessings.

Praise precedes victory. Your faith is fueled by praise in either words or song. In praise, your facial expression is bright and jubilant, and you feel wonderful and positive. You vibrate at a higher frequency that helps you to be more in tune with Source. The term *praise* has become so overused that it's lost its meaning for most people. Thanksgiving and praise don't suddenly do away with your problems or cause the heavens to open up with an outpouring of your Desire. They unconsciously raise your spirits, condition your thoughts, and set you up to receive what is already yours.

It is easy and common to praise and express gratitude after obtaining what we want, even if the outcome was not anticipated. As soon as a Desire is realized, praise follows naturally. However, not many people readily praise and offer thanks before their Desire is realized. Human beings are typically inclined to rely on their senses. When they see, feel, smell, taste, and hear, then something is real. That is when they acknowledge receipt or the realization of their Desire. I encourage you to give thanks and praise in faith. You have yet to experience or feel anything, but you continue to praise and give thanks. Blessed are those who have not yet seen, yet believe. You praise and give thanks in the joyous expectation of your Desire. Your praise fuels your faith and helps you remain connected to Source, where you want to be.

Gratitude helps maintain the high frequency you need to remain connected with Source. When you thankfully acknowledge the Giver of all good things, you maintain your focus and relationship with God. Awareness of your Source is not something you can manufacture; it is an inherent characteristic that comes with the consciousness of God. Because it encourages you to think of God as the Source of All, rather than a means or channel by which these things will come to you, it aids in the remembering that your goal is to focus on God rather than on how these things will get into your life. Knowing that God is your Source helps you avoid feelings of scarcity, because He is the God of abundance. Taking a moment to be grateful to God for what you have helps you avoid becoming obsessed with what others may have that you don't possess. This keeps competitive thoughts at bay. When you dwell on gratitude, it implies that you are expressing appreciation for something. This by itself impresses that good thing on your subconscious, and you'll have more reasons to be grateful as your subconscious will return what you impress on it.

The story of the ten lepers who were healed by the Master—Jesus Christ—is a good illustration of man's obligation to show gratitude and the value of doing so. Only one leper returned to the Master to express his gratitude for being healed of leprosy, a persistent and disfiguring skin disease. He was completely healed and made whole.

Patience is a virtue. You can obtain what you want if you believe in the process and stay committed. Everything, according to the Law of Gestation, must pass through a specific amount of time before becoming or manifesting. There is a process to follow, and it will take time. Staying focused and disciplined while following the process will help you succeed during this period. The germination, growth, and production of fruit takes place over several phases. A lack of attention and self-discipline can delay or disrupt the gestation process. The gestation period of nine months that newborns undergo before being born is another illustration. It is during this period that some individuals may get in the way of the fulfillment of their Desire. If you plant an orange seed and dig it up every few days to check on it, the seed will never grow into an orange tree and produce fruit. With patience, the process will take its course. Even if your situation does not appear to be working in your favor, maintain a good attitude, keep the faith, and trust the process.

This is where *good self-discipline* comes in handy. *You must be disciplined to follow through with the concepts outlined in this book.* And when your patience is put to the test, self-discipline becomes even more vital. The important role discipline plays cannot be ignored. It is the backbone of any success story. Without discipline, it would be difficult, if not impossible, to achieve anything worthwhile in life. The same applies to manifesting money.

Discipline is key because it allows you to stick to your goals and not get sidetracked. When you discipline yourself and make a habit of paying attention to your thoughts and words, you will find it much easier to maintain the discipline and focus that are necessary to manifest money. Discipline means exercising self-control and being able to withstand adversity and temptation, even when you do not feel like it. Success is about discipline, discipline, and discipline.

Faith is the substance of the things hoped for, the evidence of things not seen. It is the complete confidence in an outcome that you cannot see with your physical eyes. It's been said that seeing is believing, and believing is seeing. Some believe the former, and others, the latter. These two thoughts may seem like a play on words, but they are both true and necessary when it comes to manifesting or realizing any Desire you have.

Believing and seeing go hand in hand when manifesting or realizing any Desire. If you believe in the power of co-creation with God, believing is seeing whatever you desire come true! All you have to do is hold the vision in your Mind's eye and believe it with all your heart! Everything exists in the spiritual realm before it manifests into the physical world. Because you've seen it in the spiritual realm, you can be absolutely sure that you'll see it in the physical realm.

Manifesting your Desire may seem like a daunting task, but by having a little bit of faith, taking some steps toward believing and visualizing your Desire, taking action toward your goals, and believing that it's possible for you to have what you want and that you deserve it, you can make anything happen. When you believe in the power of God to bring your Desires to fruition, you will start seeing opportunities and potential for what you want all around you. You'll begin manifesting things in your life that before were only a figment of your imagination.

You already know the Universe is abundant with any good Desire. You also know that Source seeks to express through His creation, that is, you and me. As you may recall from the Law of Gestation, it's only a matter of time before your Desire is realized, as long as you adhere to the ideas in this book. To receive, you must have faith. Abraham was credited with faith because he believed in the prophecy and regarded himself to be the father of many people, despite the fact that there was no proof of his paternity. He had faith in the one who promised—Source, God. You go to school in order to obtain a certificate or degree and secure employment at the end of the course. The Word of God has integrity. It will serve you in the same way that it has served other people under similar circumstances. What you do with it is the key. In order to obtain the guarantee or bring your Desire into reality, you must act on faith. Don't allow the power of the Word to be obscured by your disbelief.

Faith drives away fear. Fear springs from negative thinking that should not be entertained or left to linger for too long. Fear may occasionally warn you about potential dangers, allowing you to avoid them. However, fear that keeps you from taking action that will enable your goal to succeed is there to steal your dreams and should not be entertained. You'll be able to overcome fear with faith.

Expectation: An expectation is a belief that something will happen or that you will get something. As long as Earth remains, there will be seed time and harvest time. Every time we put our expectation in God, He sees to it that the outcome is good. "For surely there is an end; and thine expectation shall not be cut off"—*Proverbs 23:18.*

We must understand expectation and how it works with the Law of Receiving. When we learn to expect good, all that is good comes our way, and we find that life is full of surprises. When we expect bad, we find that life is full of disappointments. Disappointments and bad luck are like a boomerang: The things you do not want, come back and hit you in the face. Therefore, it becomes vital to have expectation on God's Word. When expectation is kept on God's Word, and it is put on the things we don't see, no disappointments or bad luck will come. We must expect good and believe it is already ours and live in the joyous expectation of the manifestation of our Desire.

Don't pass up an opportunity to receive because you weren't expecting anything.

Expectation is an important aspect of receiving. What you anticipate will happen is based on reality. I'm not referring to situations where someone gives with the objective of obtaining something in return. I'm talking about the optimism in someone's heart.

But precisely, what are you expecting to receive? If you don't know what you're expecting, nothing will happen. You won't reach your goal if you don't have a destination in mind. You must be clear on your objective.

How can you tell whether you've achieved it if you don't know what your Desire is in the first place?

Others may remark, "Well, I figured it was bad luck, that I wasn't going to succeed in the first place," and so on. They are not expecting anything positive or desirable to happen. They've already announced their intention to fail. That's the firm expectation. You'll discover that when you tell yourself, "I don't recall," or "I've forgotten," you're not expecting to remember, and you've given your brain every opportunity possible to stop attempting to remember what it is that you want to remember.

While you wait for your wish to come true, get ready to receive it. This is similar to my family preparing ahead of time by storing big containers in case the rains came. Assume you wish to manifest one million dollars. At the bare minimum, you'll need to open an account at a financial institution to deposit it in. This may sound strange, but there are still many people in the United States who do not have bank accounts. According to a 2019 Federal Deposit Insurance Corporation survey, 5.4% of the U.S. population, that is, 7.1 million people, are unbanked, having no bank or credit union account.

I was fortunate to hear a pastor talk about how he and his wife of 14 years tried to have a child. After trying everything they could, they decided to buy a home and fully furnished one of the rooms as their child's nursery. Of course, some people questioned if they were going insane. But the first child arrived, followed by a second one. So, while expecting, they also prepared to receive.

It is said that the people of a village were praying for rain. The village pastor called for the villagers to congregate at the village square to pray for rain. He requested that everyone bring a symbol of their faith. Some people brought their Bibles, others crucifixes, and other religious objects. A little nine-year-old brought an umbrella, and some laughed at him for such a senseless token. They prayed, and sure enough, the rain began to fall. When asked why he brought an umbrella, he responded that he came to pray in faith and was confident that his request would be granted, so he brought one.

Have you started looking at houses in the area where you want to buy if you wish to purchase a new property using the money you manifest? Have you started to research the industry and conduct a market analysis if you want to start a business? Have you established any eligibility criteria for a scholarship foundation if your Desire is to develop a scholarship program? Have you started to build the network and seek endorsements if you aspire to run for public office?

"Ask, and it shall be given you; seek, and ye shall find; knock, and it shall be opened unto you:

For every one that asketh receiveth; and he that seeketh findeth; and to him that knocketh it shall be opened"—Matthew 7:7-8. In your asking, what will you take as your token of faith?

You must take action. You might be wondering, "What should I do now? Do I have to take any action? I thought all I had to do was visualize my Desire, make some money affirmations, give freely and generously and keep the faith, and the money would come to me." You're correct in assuming that, and you must follow along with all of the other suggestions made here. You see, at the very least, you must go outside and set your container to collect the rainwater that is flowing freely for you. The Internet is replete with so-called easy ways to make money; however, some action is still required. I don't mean working yourself to the bone. Just like with anything else in life, you will get out what you put in. You can't just sit around thinking about what you want and expect it to happen. If you truly desire something, are prepared to implement the concepts in this book, and are willing to do what it takes, then Source will orchestrate everything in your favor to make it happen effortlessly.

Follow your vision into action. According to Wallace D. Wattles, "By thought, the thing you want is brought to you; by action you receive it." Faith without work is dead. You must supplement everything I've said in this book with your actions. *You must act immediately and consistently.* You change things when you believe with your whole heart and see everything through the eyes of faith. When you view things with the eyes of faith, opportunities to fulfill your goals are revealed to you. You must take immediate action on what has been revealed to you.

When you take action on your dreams and goals, the Universe will take action too; every cause has an effect. You take action on your dreams when you take the necessary steps to actualize them. Putting faith into action is like putting money in the bank; it starts to accumulate through interest.

You may be introduced to famous personal finance and money experts and their programs, such as Dave Ramsey's Financial Peace University, Ric Edelman's Financial Engines, Loral Langemeier's Integrated Wealth Systems, Robert Kiyosaki's Rich Dad Poor Dad, and others. You may also discover some investment companies that can help you use your money to generate income and make your money work for you. I mention these experts because of my personal experience using their services or programs. You could be asked to have lunch with Warren Buffett and pick up a multimillion dollar business idea. You might finally get the chance to promote your product or business concept on television, perhaps on a well-known show such as *Shark Tank*, or be offered the chance to join a startup firm. It may be an idea to buy into a franchise system or start your business independently. It may be beneficial to take a course at a school or work with a coach. As a coach, my goal is to help individuals in utilizing their natural talents and abilities to manifest their Desires. It may include elements of any of the above or other ideas.

When these ideas and opportunities are revealed to you, take immediate action, but bear in mind that Source will not provide you with inspiration or opportunities that are out of line with His nature. God will not reveal to you any ideas to rob a bank and steal a million dollars. If you're really in harmony with Source, such notions won't spring to mind.

Let's look at the scenario of manifesting one million dollars again. Assume you've checked off all of the boxes, adhered to each principle, visualized it, and you are certain it's a done deal. As you continue, your spirit will be receptive to ideas, possibilities, and connections that you'll need to implement in order to manifest this Desire. Pay close attention as you visualize, meditate, and praise. Keep a journal of your ideas and actions. Some of these may appear to be far-fetched, and you may begin to doubt how they will be realized. Remember, the how is not up to you; it's up to Source. Infinite Source has the ability to bring resources to you in the least expected way. Source may order the actions of others to favor you or come to your aid, so take the first step in faith. Don't let fear take control. It will steal your Desire if you don't fight it. Continue to repeat your affirmations and offer encouraging words and ideas to your Subconscious Mind.

Don't brush aside the ideas. For whatever reason, a seemingly straightforward idea might be disregarded or neglected because it fails to meet your expectations. Naaman was a king who had a skin disease. His Desire was to be healed of this condition. Well, a certain prophet instructed him to bathe himself in the River Jordan seven times in order to cleanse his skin. He dismissed it as a crazy notion. Fortunately for him, his wife's servant persuaded him to try it, and when he did, his Desire was fulfilled.

It's possible that, in taking action, you'll need to provide services to others. How you go about obtaining what you desire is critical to your ability to receive it. Always render such services with honesty and integrity, providing more value to those you serve than what they pay for your services. In other words, don't deceive or take advantage of others. In the process of increasing others, you will experience increase.

You must develop unwavering persistence for what you want until you get the desired results. In taking action, the importance of persistence cannot be overemphasized. Many people have been able to manifest money by persistence, hard work, and focus. However, it is important to note that persistence with regard to manifestation doesn't necessarily mean doing the same thing over and over again until you get what you want or not stopping until you collapse. Sometimes persistence means faith and determination plus taking certain actions at the right time to bring about the desired results; allowing your persistent thoughts to guide your way; keeping yourself charged up emotionally about getting what you desire most in life; and staying determined with your plan toward success.

Here are some tips to help you remain persistent:

You must have complete clarity about your Desire and a burning passion for it. You must believe that the money is already yours. Affirm this belief every day until it becomes a reality. Then focus on the end result, not the process. Don't get sidetracked by challenges or get bogged down by the details; just stay focused on the Desire.

When thinking of positioning yourself or preparing to receive, think of a goalkeeper during a soccer game. There is, in fact, an art to goalkeeping. The eyes should be on the ball at all times, and both feet should be shoulder-width apart. To effectively take advantage of this type of play, your brain and body must be prepared to spring into action at a moment's notice. The goalkeeper understands that eventually the ball will come his way. It may appear that they are simply standing there doing nothing, but this isn't the case. The goalkeeper's attention is completely focused on catching the ball when it comes hurtling toward the goal during the games, whether it's passed from one player to another or bounces off a post or crossbar. After all the tedious training, coaching, warmup sessions, and so on, it's time for the goalkeeper to react swiftly and act.

There will be challenges along the way, but keep in mind this old saying: "The same boiling water that softens the potato hardens the egg. It's about what you're made of, not the circumstances." Remember your origin and the Truth about who you are. Whatever you desire, position yourself to receive it, since Source has a far greater Desire to offer you even more than you could ever imagine. The Word of God is Truth, and it will never change. It's time to get rid of the beliefs that have kept you from experiencing the abundance of money in the Universe.

Chapter 9 Exercise: Old versus New Beliefs

Remember the Desires you wrote down in chapter five? Now, identify and summarize the top three ideas presented in this chapter that may help you prepare or be better positioned to receive at least one of them.

_____

_____

_____

_____

_____

_____

_____

_____

_____

_____

_____

_____

_____

_____

_____

_____

_____

_____

_____

_____

_____

_____

_____

CHAPTER 10

From Your Mind to Your Hand

This last chapter is a collection of some practical and highly effective tools to assist you on your manifestation journey—the journey from your Mind to your hands in the shortest and most effortless way possible. It is intended to offer you some direction and a head start in applying the principles presented in this book. The consistent application of these useful tools will not only assist you to attract money into your life but will also aid in the accelerated manifestation of any Desire.

At this point, you should have more than enough practical knowledge to be able to start manifesting your Desires. I am confident that some of the things you read here will resonate with your real-life experience. Although some may still seem foreign, keep an open mind since all of these techniques are effective. If even one or two of these practical tools can assist you in manifesting money into your life, the entire book was well worth reading!

These practical tools can be used in conjunction with the exercises included in this book or on their own. Keep in mind that the manifestation of your Desire will take some time; any process requires time to reach its optimum outcome. If you follow the instructions carefully, it is quite likely that you will see amazing results sooner than you probably anticipated; however, be sure to complete every exercise as they are intended to work synergistically to assist you with your manifestation objectives.

Manifestation Puzzle

You've probably heard the popular quotation, "Life is like a jigsaw puzzle." I agree, and manifesting anything you desire is very similar. It's only when all the puzzle pieces are connected or linked together that the magnificent masterpiece emerges. Every piece is essential and must fit correctly for the manifestation of your Desire. This is what I call the *Manifestation Puzzle—the masterpiece within the pieces.*

Throughout the book, we've touched on many aspects of the puzzle, and now is a great time to put them all together. I enjoy working on puzzles, even though I don't get to do so very often. I try to avoid glancing at the completed picture on the cover too frequently since it detracts from the excitement. When looking for a part, it's not unusual to become discouraged, especially if the puzzle is complex and there are many small pieces. It may take somewhat longer at such times, and I just want to stop. However, having my attention fixed on the final picture, I redouble my efforts, and at last the masterpiece is revealed. Just like a goalkeeper would, keep your eye focused on the ball, your Desire, that which you would love to manifest.

When solving a puzzle, you may find yourself stumped as to which piece to start with and which piece to continue with, among other things. For some puzzles, putting the edges together first is a popular technique, but it isn't applicable to all puzzles. Just as there is really no prescribed way or a single overriding strategy for solving every puzzle, where you start in the Manifestation Puzzle is very personal. It all depends on where you're at in the process of bringing your Desire into reality.

As you come to the end of this book, you could be asking yourself, "Where do I begin?" Everyone is at a different point in life with his or her own set of circumstances and beliefs. To manifest your Desire, you must first figure out where to start and what to do next. As a destiny coach and mentor, I can guide you to develop a personalized approach that will help you put your own unique pieces together. Your Desire is visualized as a picture in your Mind. Putting the pieces of the puzzle together will result in your Desire coming into being or materializing in your hands.

A balance of determination, discipline, persistence, and patience is needed to bring your ideas together in order to manifest money or other Desires in your life. There may be moments when you are uncertain about what to do next. Alternatively, you might believe that you are not making any progress, and it is time to call it quits. On other days, however, you may get sidetracked, causing everything to fall apart, and you have to start all over. These times will necessitate you looking at the picture of the puzzle you're attempting to put together and being inspired and motivated to continue.

The Manifestation Puzzle—The Masterpiece Within the Pieces

Let's take a closer look at the puzzle pieces that make up the masterpiece.

Awareness: Socrates said, "You don't know what you don't know." You can't get the most out of what you don't realize you have. Become aware of your true self, and look at things from a different perspective.

Abundance: The limitless and perpetually increasing supply of Source. Relegate fear and unhealthy competition to the dustbin; there is more than enough for you.

Love: Everything is done out of a love for God, oneself, and others. God is love. A Desire generated by love is inherently good.

Alignment: Vibrate at a frequency that keeps you aligned with Source.

Words: Flip the script and use the right words. Have a childlike trust in the power of the Word. Choose your words carefully and speak wisely, in accordance with the Word.

Thoughts: Think on things that condition your Mind and beliefs in a positive way. Consider how you may use your Mind and beliefs to construct a better reality. Are your thoughts in harmony with Source?

Visualization: Look with your Mind's eye. Look at things from a new perspective, and keep that vision in mind.

Visualization board: Create a physical representation of your Desire. It will assist you in keeping the vision alive.

Manifestation Puzzle

Feelings: You must feel it to manifest it. Feel the joy of already having your Desire fulfilled.

Desire: What would you love, and how strong and clear is your Desire?

Goal card: Keep your goals close at hand for constant reminders, inspiration, and motivation.

Mindset: Renew your Mind. Set your Mind on things that keep you connected to Source.

Beliefs: Replace any limiting or negative ideas (paradigms) that are preventing you from manifesting your Desires

Switching techniques: There will be challenges, so use your switching techniques to stay connected to Source.

Meditation: Meditation helps you attain a high frequency and connect with the energy of Source.

Sleep: The temporary loss of consciousness, during which the subconscious creative aspect of your Mind takes over. Give your Mind something to work on that is consistent with your Desire, and allow it enough time to do its creative job.

Giving: Giving is its own reward. Giving is receiving; as you give, so shall you receive.

Gratitude: Keep a grateful demeanor and attitude. You already have everything you could want in the spiritual realm. Gratitude is a form of public declaration that you have what you want.

Praise: Praise precedes victory. Praise fuels your faith.

Faith: With faith all things are possible. Exercise unwavering faith.

Prayer: In this case, prayer is not about the asking as much as it is about humility and reverence. Humble yourself in praise and worship as you focus on Source.

Affirmations: Use your money affirmations constantly to impress the right thoughts on your Subconscious Mind. Repetition is key.

Truth: Don't confuse Facts for Truth. Let Truth be your guide.

Action: Take action, in faith and with purpose. You have to be willing to put in the work if you want to see results. Take immediate action on the ideas that come to Mind, and visualize, praise, and meditate when you wake up in the morning.

Patience: You may not see the results you Desire right away, but with patience and tenacity, you will eventually achieve them. Don't get discouraged if you don't see results immediately. Focus on what you want rather than what you don't want, remain positive and optimistic throughout the process, and believe in the manifestation of your Desire. The sooner you believe in the realization of your Desire, the sooner it will manifest.

Persistence: The ability to stay on track despite challenges is something everyone needs in order to stay true to their dreams and see their Desires realized. It's not giving up in the face of adversity, even when things don't go according to plan. Believe in yourself, take action, and celebrate successes, no matter how small.

Discipline: It is giving yourself a command and following it. It's your ability to stay committed to your goal and the actions necessary to make it happen. Make a point of doing what you set out to do, no matter what.

This Manifestation Puzzle is a puzzle game to assist you in manifesting any wonderful Desire you can visualize (see page 159).

Mind Management

Be kind to your Mind. Your Mind is the instrument and mechanism through which Source has endowed you with the ability to translate and appropriate your Desires from the spiritual realm into the physical world. We're continuously preoccupied with what we'll wear, how we'll look, what we'll eat, and so on. But do we ever stop to think about our Mind? How frequently do we give our thoughts any attention? Mind Management is a lot more complicated than that, but I hope at the very least that this resource will help you begin to consider your Mind and focus on your thoughts. Remember, "As a man thinketh so is he." Your creative ideas can be fueled by this Mind Management strategy, which helps you concentrate on your thoughts. It will assist in the manifestation of your Desire by fostering a healthy and successful Mind.

Mind Management is a fantastic tool for learning how to use your Mind to improve all aspects of your life. It's not just about money, though; it's also about time management, goal-setting skills, and so much more! When you master this secret technique for manifesting anything you want, it'll give you an advantage and put you ahead of the curve when it comes to manifesting anything you Desire.

PREMIERE DESTINY
UNLOCK YOUR DESTINY

MIND MANAGEMENT PLAN
FOR MANIFESTING MONEY

Goal	Duration	Description
SPRING CLEAN YOUR MIND	2-4 WEEKS	Get rid of hatred, unforgiveness, anger. These cannot align with Love.
REWNEW YOUR MIND	4 WEEKS	Feed your Mind with Truth based on the Word of God. You are a co-creator with Source. Prosperity is your inheritance.
CLEARLY DEFINED INTENTION	2 WEEKS	Use the power of visualization to clearly define your desire. Clarity aides the subconscious mind.
RESPECT & LOVE MONEY	3-4 WEEKS	Replace negative money beliefs with daily money affirmations. Love of money must not supersede the love of God.
STAY POSITIVE	2-3 WEEKS	Focus on positive thoughts and activities that uplift your spirit.
TAP INTO YOUR INTUITION	4 WEEKS	Learn to hear the gentle and calm, yet confident inner voice. Inspired action may come through your intuition.
LEARN TO TRUST SOURCE	3-4 WEEKS	Cast all your cares on Him and be anxious for nothing. Anxiety does not favor money manifestation.

Adjust the duration of each goal to suit your circumstances. For example: As you read this book, you may have already started getting rid of negative money beliefs. This may reduce the time for accomplishing that goal from 3-4 weeks to 1-2 weeks.

WWW.PREMIEREDESTINY.COM

Mind Management

Affirmation Calendar

Develop a new, positive, and healthy relationship with money by utilizing the 31-day affirmation program. Focus on one affirmation at a time each day, repeating it several times throughout the day.

Repetition is key! As you repeat these affirmations daily, you will gradually but surely discard any and all negative money beliefs while also refreshing your Mind and developing a new and beneficial relationship with money.

PREMIERE DESTINY
UNLOCK YOUR DESTINY

AFFIRMATION CALENDAR
31 DAYS OF MONEY AFFIRMATIONS

Declare what you desire right now, despite any current limiting or negative beliefs or circumstances that may be standing in your path.

1 I release any and all negative energy about money.	**2** I am at peace with desiring and having more money.	**3** I am born rich.	**4** I am connected to an endless supply of money.	**5** I have more than enough money to be a blessing to others.	**6** Money is God at work in and through me.	**7** The Lord is my Shepard; I shall not want.
8 I am a conduit of God's abundance.	**9** I experience an abundant flow of money in my life.	**10** I have a wonderful relationship with money.	**11** Money comes to me increasingly.	**12** I am living a supernaturally wealthy lifestyle.	**13** I stand in Faith that all my financial needs are met.	**14** I owe nothing to anyone except my obligation to love them.
15 I have multiple sources of income.	**16** I have the ability to create wealth.	**17** Money comes to me on a continuous basis.	**18** I use money to improve the lives of others.	**19** Money located me for every good cause.	**20** I take actions that create more money for me.	**21** I have more money to cover my expenses.
22 I know how to manage and invest my money.	**23** I am debt free.	**24** Money is energy and it flows to me easily.	**25** I love money and money loves me.	**26** I put money to good use.	**27** I give money generously and it comes back to me multiplied.	**28** I am Divinely supplied so I lack nothing.
29 I enjoy the prosperous life that money affords me.	**30** I am grateful for the money I have.	**31** I have a beautiful and lasting relationship with money.		Visit www.moneylocatesyou.com		

Affirmation Calendar

Seven Proven Bedtime Manifestation Routines

A powerful time for creating is during sleep. This is because your Subconscious Mind is most open to suggestion then. The day's events are behind you, and the stillness of night gives your Conscious Mind a break. When you're asleep, your inner self has free rein to create what it wants for the future. Even if you haven't had time to plan this out consciously, your subconscious will still do its best to make it happen.

Developing a winning bedtime routine is a must for manifestation. It's conceivable that your habits are the source of your problems if you're having difficulties in realizing your Desire. Practicing these bedtime routines will help your Subconscious Mind get on board with what you're trying to do, supporting and lining up with your Desire. A consistent bedtime helps your Subconscious Mind to make solid connections with your Desire.

Before going to sleep at night, visualize what you want as if it has already been achieved—just relax and spend time with your Mind-Body, seeing this as reality. (In other words, feel like these things are real now.)

Closing your eyes and picturing all the things you want to manifest into your life, preferably in stages, aids in memory recall of what you're saying yes to as well as a sort of mental rehearsal before the new day begins.

These seven tried-and-true bedtime routines are straightforward to follow, and they can help you develop success habits that will assist you in bringing your Desire into reality.

7 PROVEN BEDTIME MANIFESTATION ROUTINES

SLEEP: YOUR NATURAL STATE FOR CREATION
A SELF PACED GUIDE FOR CREATING DURING SLEEP

GRATITUDE
QUIETLY FOCUS ON WHAT YOU ARE GRATEFUL FOR NOW

TIP: Focus on one or two things you are grateful for today.

MEDITATE
MEDITATE ON YOUR DESIRE

TIP: Write out your desire. Choose a personalized affirmation from the affirmation calendar to focus on.

UP YOUR VIBRATION
FALL ASLEEP FEELING GOOD

TIP: Avoid negative images or information that may disturb your sleep.

VISUALIZE
SEE YOURSELF HAVING YOUR DESIRE AS YOU FALL ASLEEP

TIP: Use your visualization board or goal card.

SLEEP
GIVE YOUR SUBCONSCIOUS MIND UNINTERRUPTED AND MAXIMUM TIME TO GO TO WORK FOR YOU.

TIP: Ideal sleep temperature is 68 degrees F.

WRITE DOWN IDEAS
JOT DOWN ANY CREATIVE IDEAS THAT CAME TO YOUR CONSCIOUSNESS AS YOU WOKE UP

TIP: Keep pen and paper handy to write. Write before getting out of bed.

PRAISE BEFORE YOU GO
THIS HELPS YOU FOCUS ON POSITIVE THOUGHTS DURING THE COURSE OF THE DAY.

TIP: praise must have content. Start by thanking God for waking up from sleep today.

PREMIEREDESTINY.COM

7 Proven Bedtime Routines

Feelings—How are you feeling?

Your feelings dictate your vibrational frequency. *You must feel it to receive it.*

Feelings are the manifestation of one's thoughts and beliefs, which in turn influence the manifestation of any Desire. Your feelings are the emotional energy dominating your Mind at any given time. The intensity of this emotional energy becomes the signal that attracts the circumstances and serves as the trigger for bringing about your Desire. As a result, it's critical that your emotions remain in balance and aligned with your Desire. All good Desires originate from Source. The more expanded your emotions, the closer and more aligned they are to Source, resulting in an effortless manifestation of your Desire.

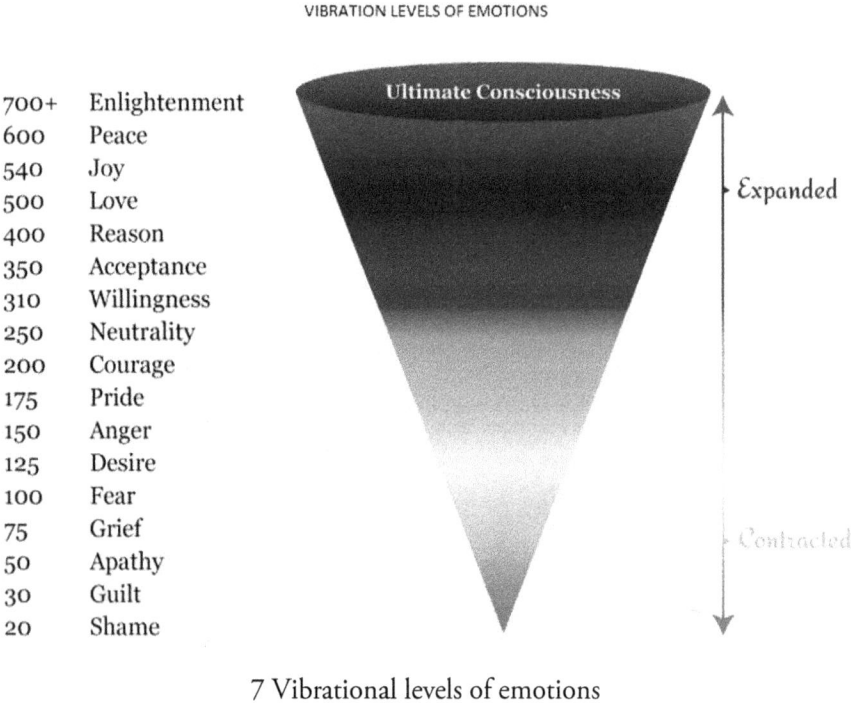

VIBRATION LEVELS OF EMOTIONS

700+	Enlightenment
600	Peace
540	Joy
500	Love
400	Reason
350	Acceptance
310	Willingness
250	Neutrality
200	Courage
175	Pride
150	Anger
125	Desire
100	Fear
75	Grief
50	Apathy
30	Guilt
20	Shame

Ultimate Consciousness

Expanded

Contracted

7 Vibrational levels of emotions

Manifestation Road Map

And finally, this visual of the manifestation road map is a synopsis of the ideas in this book in a step-by-step approach to guide you on your manifestation journey. As you faithfully take these steps with commitment and the joyous expectation to receive, money will locate you for any good Desire.

Manifestation Road Map

A guide to manifesting any good desire.

See Differently

Awareness of truth brings about a new and different reality. Be open minded to seeing things from a new perspective, through your mind's eye and hold on to that vision.

Think Differently

With a new outlook on life and possibilities, change your beliefs, thoughts and renew your mind to promote the right vibrational frequencies.

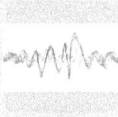

Feel Differently

Feeling is receiving. As you visualize, hold that vision of already realizing your desire. The direction of your emotions must be towards ultimate consciousness.

Speak Differently

Your words have the power of life and death. Speak your desire to life by maintaining positive daily affirmations.

Act Differently

Supplement your thoughts, feelings and words with immediate personal action. Action must be in faith and purpose leaving every person with a feeling of increase.

Manifest Differently

Be ready to receive your desire and stay in a state of joyous expectation. Your results are sure to leave you in awe.

premieredestiny.com

Manifestation Road Map

Conclusion

—————— ～ ——————

I t is mind-boggling that many of us do not enjoy the abundance of the Universe, not because we consciously choose not to, but simply because we lack awareness. And even when we become aware, our good old paradigms and negative beliefs tend to act as a restraining force, holding us back from accepting, believing, and letting Truth become our new reality. Changing ingrained, long-held views and beliefs about money might appear to be a straightforward and simple process, but it will require serious resolve, continued practice, and discipline. Sometimes you really do have to fake it till you make it. You see, as Bob Proctor said, "It is not who you are that holds you back, it's who you think you're not."

The laws and principles discussed in this book are based on Truth, the Truth of the Word of God. Truth is superior to Facts, and it is unchanging and unfailing; it is Infinite Intelligence. Embracing Truth will help you renew your Mind and change the way you see, think, feel, speak, and act.

Every living thing must remain connected to its Source. You originated from God, from His Spirit, and you must remain connected to the Spirit of Source. When you do, you'll live a successful life of abundance. When you believe that there is such a life, you must then live according to the principles or laws of that life. Anything short of that restricts the manifestation of the expected lifestyle of abundance. Do not limit God. With your Mind's eyes, see what you desire, and stay aligned with Source. You become that channel or conduit of manifestation, and you manifest your wishes supernaturally if you remain connected, aligned with Source, as Neville Goddard says, the effortless way. Yes, money will locate you.

They that know their God, shall do great exploits. They are conscious of His ever-present Grace, His ability in them. They believe in *John 16:1 5* that says, "All things that the Father hath are mine." Infinite Intelligence, the Universal Mind, God, is always with us and responds to our faith, irrespective of the circumstances. Don't pass up God because you were caught up in the distractions of the world through your senses. Don't limit what God can do by your human understanding. Be steadfast in the Word. Maintain your affirmations by keeping your thoughts focused on the Word, which is the Truth. Remember that there is something in you, beyond your human understanding. It is supernatural. You have a part to play in the manifestation of your Desire. However, remember, it is not by your power nor by your might, but by the Spirit of God. Our faith does not stand in the wisdom of man but the dynamic might of God, which enables us to accomplish what it promises. You are not ordinary; you are a co-creator with the Source of All.

Where you are in life today is a result of your level of awareness. Whatever you're attracting in your life is also a result of your level of awareness. Your current salary (or profit for business owners) is also a result of your level of awareness. You may make $85,000 per year if you are not aware that you can earn more than $85,000 per month. This was the experience of a registered nurse, and it may be yours as well.

This very book you are now reading is a concrete example of a strong Desire and proof of the integrity and efficacy of the ideas, principles, and laws in this book. It is a product of the product. If there's any question in your Mind, in your hands is proof. I was completely unaware of how and when the Desire was going to manifest. I must have been aligned with Source after my praise session as I stepped out of the shower in May 2021. The title of the book popped into my consciousness, immediately followed by a strong Desire to write a book about it. The amazing thing about the entire book-writing process is that I had never even remotely considered writing a book before. Teaching, mentoring, and coaching others for success I do and enjoy. I've now fallen in love with writing, and I'm having a great time through each step of the way to publishing this book.

Many people search for answers in a variety of places and put forth their best efforts to bring their Desires to reality, yet the manifestation of their Desires remains elusive. Many "Amens!" and "I receive!" become shattered hopes and abandoned dreams and aspirations, and despair takes over. The idea that life will suddenly improve, or that the world will suddenly change, becomes a lie. That would not be the case if we were aware of who we truly are and remained connected to Source. Live from the consciousness of the Truth of your oneness with God and that you are a co-creator with God and a channel of the ever-increasing and fuller expression of His abundance. Your level of consciousness of yourself explains your life's circumstances. A single orange seed contains the potential to produce hundreds of oranges. Regardless of how much this orange seed desires additional oranges, it must be connected to its Source (the ground) for its Desire to become a reality. All the laws mentioned in this book point back to Source, the I AM THAT I AM—the Unchanging, Creative Source of All. Without an awareness of one's spiritual origin and purpose, one's self-awareness is incomplete. Life is spiritual; therefore, life needs to be understood in terms of spirituality. When we are in alignment with Source, the manifestation of that which does not appear into that which does, becomes feasible and even effortless.

Let your Mind be open to the ideas shared with you here, because they will work for you if followed correctly, and now that you are aware of them, allow yourself to accept them. My own experiences thus far are testimonies to the fact that these ideas and principles are capable of extraordinary things for you and through you. But you must be ready to accept them as true, keep the good intentions of your heart, and tap into and draw from the limitless and unchangeable Source of All.

There are no single principles or laws that may be used by themselves; they're all linked. Take a look at it as a whole package rather than focusing on one aspect. You won't perceive the whole picture until you've connected all of the pieces of a puzzle. I hope that the Manifestation Puzzle will assist you in manifesting money in your life, which you never believed or hoped was possible. Source wants money to locate you. It is not His Desire for you to be poor or broke. He created you in His image and after His own likeness. In alignment, you're an extension of Source. In and through you, His ever-increasing beauty is expressed and manifested. In alignment, there is oneness; His Desires are your Desires, and your Desires are His Desires. What He Desires, He makes possible. He makes money locate those who are aligned and positioned to act in faith and with purpose. He has provided you with all you require to live a successful and prosperous life, including His Word, your Mind, your mouth, and your hands. Renew your Mind with the right thoughts, affirm words of Truth, be ready to take inspired action, and money will locate you for any good Desire because *money is God in action in and through you.*

After reading this whole book, are you ready to receive what God has to offer? All good things are waiting for you—right now! You can have anything that your heart desires. The only question is, "What would you love?"

A commitment to believe and apply all the ideas explained in this book will prove right the main premise of this book: Source is seeking to express His abundance through anyone who is aligned with Him. Why not you?

About the Author

Joan Ekobena is a visionary and an entrepreneur with an inspiring, heart-touching story. She's an inspirational and motivational speaker, mentor, and coach. Joan's life has truly been a story of living her dreams by following her heart's desires.

Joan is a mother of three and a wife with a diverse professional background in banking, finance, information technology, and nursing. Most notably, Joan has served in healthcare as CEO of her company for the past twenty years, serving and advocating on television for the elderly.

Joan has always had a deep sense of compassion for others and an intense interest in discovering how you can excel in whatever you do for the good of all involved. She mentors individuals on personal development and spiritual growth, as well as advises companies on strategic and operational success.

Joan strongly believes that everyone has the innate ability to achieve any goal they set their mind to—it's just a matter of awareness and changing beliefs and behaviors to get there!

This belief drives Joan's desire to help people unveil, harness, and bring out the best of themselves so they can live life on their own terms, lives of uncommon success, and become the designers of their destinies.

Stemming from childhood experiences and subsequent insights as an adult, Joan is passionate about money and guiding others into an awareness of experiencing it from a standpoint of abundance.

Premiere Destiny

www.PremiereDestiny.com

Premiere Destiny is dedicated to serving and empowering individuals around the world, by raising their vibrational frequency through mindset growth, personal development, and spiritual guidance.

With the dedicated guidance of Bob Proctor and Peggy McColl, Joan and Paul have achieved quantum leaps in their own lives and now they are committed to helping you achieve yours!

The Premiere Destiny team are certified Destiny Coaches, passionate about working with individuals, like yourself, to uncover the lessons of the ages that are contained within Peggy McColl's Destiny Key and Money Marathon programs.

Premiere Destiny's special, unique, & intensive approach will inspire and instruct "everyday" individuals, entrepreneurs, and authors to reach their maximum potential and truly unlock their own destiny.

To explore all the ways in which Premiere Destiny can help you unveil, harness, and bring out the best in you, so you can be the designer of your own destiny, book your complimentary Discovery Call by visiting:

http://www.calendly.com/premieredestiny/

For more information on what Premiere Destiny has to offer, please visit:

www.premieredestiny.com

The Manifestation Puzzle

"If you can imagine it in your mind, you can hold it in your hand."

Joan Ekobena

It is our mission to help you fully understand and appreciate the incredible power your mind has when it comes to manifesting anything you desire.

The first step to manifesting is to create and hold in your mind a crystal clear image of what it is you truly desire. Once you have that image, you will be able to become emotionally and vibrationally aligned with what it is you want.

We have created *The Manifestation Puzzle* to help you clearly visualize the image of what you desire. Whether you are looking to manifest your soulmate, your dream home, money and wealth, or your dream vacation, we have the perfect puzzle for you.

The goal of putting the puzzle together is not just to get the final product, which is your desired image, but also what happens to you and precisely, your mind while attempting to assemble it and studying the word on each puzzle piece.

We hope the thrill of seeing your desire come true is greater than the pleasure you'll get from putting it together.

Please visit www.PremiereDestiny.com to learn more!

HEARTS to be HEARD

Giving a Voice to Creativity!

With every donation, a voice will be given to the creativity that lies within the hearts of our children living with diverse challenges.

By making this difference, children that may not have been given the opportunity to have their Heart Heard will have the freedom to create beautiful works of art and musical creations.

Donate by visiting

HeartstobeHeard.com

We thank you.

The eyes of all look to you, and you give them their
food at the proper time.

You open your hand and satisfy the
desires of every living thing.

The Lord is righteous in all his ways and
faithful in all he does.

The Lord is near to all who call on him,
to all who call on him in truth.

Psalm 145:15-18

www.ingramcontent.com/pod-product-compliance
Lightning Source LLC
Chambersburg PA
CBHW072347200326
41519CB00015B/3688